P9-DIE-381

The Church On Purpose

Keys to Effective Church Leadership

by Joe S. Ellis

STANDARD PUBLISHING
Cincinnati, Ohio   88584

Textbooks by Standard Publishing:

The Christian Minister
    Sam E. Stone
Introduction to Christian Education
    Eleanor Daniel, John W. Wade, Charles Gresham
Ministering to Youth
    David Roadcup, editor
The Church On Purpose
    Joe S. Ellis

Commentary on Acts
    J. W. McGarvey
The Equipping Ministry
    Paul Benjamin
Essays on New Testament Christianity
    C. Robert Wetzel, editor
The Fourfold Gospel
    J. W. McGarvey and P. Y. Pendleton
The Jesus Years
    Thomas D. Thurman
How to Understand the Bible
    Knofel Staton
The New Testament Church/Then and Now
    E. LeRoy Lawson
Teach With Success
    Guy P. Leavitt, revised by Eleanor Daniel

Library of Congress Cataloging in Publication Data

Ellis, Joe S.
    The church on purpose.

    Includes index.
    1. Church renewal. 2. Christian leadership. I. Title.
BV600.2.E56   262'.14   82-3175
ISBN 0-87239-441-7   AACR2

Except where otherwise specified, Scripture quotations are from the New International Version of the Bible, © 1978, New York International Bible Society.

Published by The STANDARD PUBLISHING Company, Cincinnati, Ohio.
A division of STANDEX INTERNATIONAL Corporation. Printed in U.S.A.

Foreword

Here is one of the most helpful books I have read in recent years.

Dr. Joe Ellis knows American Christians are living in the midst of the greatest revolution ever to engulf the human race. Everything is in the process of change. But, as he so firmly and so truly says everything the church does must be geared to "the accomplishment of *God's* purposes." These, at the highest level, do not change, but the means for achieving these purposes at lower levels, under today's conditions, do change. Indeed, since God wants His eternal purposes carried out, He certainly wants methods that used to work in 1850, but no longer do so, *changed*. We must carry out God's will by methods that will work in today's and tomorrow's world. The ethnic church, resolved to remain ethnic, is quite a different proposition from an ethnic church that is resolved to become an English-speaking congregation as rapidly as possible. In both congregations, God's eternal, unchanging mandates must be carried out, but by quite different methods.

Dr. Ellis writes out of a vast experience of the American churches. He describes congregations so accurately that the reader exclaims: "Of course—this is exactly the kind of a congregation we visited last summer." Dr. Ellis's far-reaching discussion of change is intensely practical. He is talking about realities faced by ministers, elders, deacons, or good Christian women of ordinary American congregations. He describes the problems precisely and suggests effective ways of changing them.

He insists that the church has an unchanging purpose—to carry out God's will as revealed in the Bible. He also insists that the way or ways of carrying out these purposes must change with every social, economic, political, and educational development in the general community.

Among many strong chapters, the one I like best is Chapter 4, entitled, "Equipping the People." This is the heart of the matter. We must form congregations of God's people who are equipped to recognize the difficulties of accomplishing God's will, agree on feasible solutions, and commit themselves to work these out. We must have congregations resolved to do God's will in this community, at this time, under these circumstances, and with the resources God has given this cell of His body.

The most important chapter in the book is Chapter 6, entitled, "Spiritual Power." Here Dr. Ellis calls our attention to the supreme purpose of God, namely, that the good news of salvation be proclaimed to every man, woman, boy, and girl, and as many as possible be brought into obedient faithful relation to the sovereign Lord. Speaking of the church, Ellis writes: "God gave it the task of making men and women disciples of His Son through the complementary processes of evangelism and edification." Again he says: "The gospel is the power of God for the salvation of everyone who believes; . . . Those who are most engaged in bringing the gospel with all its power into the lives of others, become more fully partakers of that power themselves."

In an America where the opportunities for church growth were never brighter, in a nation where there are more winnable people than ever before, *recognition of this central purpose of God* (the multiplication of Christians and congregations) must possess pastors, leaders and the whole membership if God's purpose in this great land is to be achieved. We need a much bigger spiritual majority if we are to have the votes and the muscle and the quiet Christian influence in factory, office, home, school, university, and political party that we so desperately need. Christ's command is so clear to disciple all the ethnic units *(panta ta ethne)*, all the neighborhoods, organizations, suburbs, labor unions, pleasure resorts, research associations, and on and on, that *nothing but a mighty emphasis on the Great Commission is going to achieve it.* Otherwise, we Christians will remain as we are today, a minority, desperately trying to hold on to Biblical principles in a world where the mass media, the business apparatus, the political and economic structures, and the state educational system all tend to produce a secular, if not a pagan, social order.

Dr. Ellis is right. We must have an unshakable resolve to accomplish God's purposes. Among these purposes, that of enrolling and maturing *millions* of non-Christians and nominal Christians will remain a chief and irreplaceable one.

Order several copies of this book. Read it carefully. Pass it on to responsible men, women, elders, deacons in the congregation. Let them also read it as they work to bring about change, which is so greatly needed in so many churches here in the United States of America. It is not to be supposed that no changes at all are taking place. They are taking place all the time, and will continue to take place. However, the processes of change can be made very much better, more accelerated, and more efficient than they are at present. If this book achieves that end, it will have made one of the great contributions of the 1980's to church renewal and church extension here in North America.

> *Donald McGavran*
> *Fuller Theological Seminary*
> *Pasadena, California*

Contents

Introduction

The church is in one of the most strangely mixed periods of its history. The picture is full of contradictions—patches of light and shadow, changing kaleidoscopically.

In full awareness of the axiom that "all generalizations are false," including this one—some observations, nevertheless, may be made regarding the situation in which we find ourselves.

A philosophy of despair has settled over the non-Christian world. Man's half-gods have failed him, leaving a vacuum ready to be filled with the gospel. Will Durant, perceptive historian, prophetically described these times as resembling those that "hungered for the birth of Christ." It is a time of ferment. But it is also a time of opportunity; when foundations are shaken, doors often fly open unexpectedly. Our time has been described as the greatest opportunity for the church in this century.

There is a stirring in the church and in individual lives. If such a stirring is to lead to significant results, believers "must be aware that our Lord Jesus Christ is standing in the shadows beside this ridiculous world scene, patiently waiting for His Little Children to put away their silly religious toys and programs and discover that He has come to control their mundane, pressured existences."*

More and more people are seeking a dynamic spiritual life.
Doctrinal correctness is not enough; correct doctrine does not
satisfy if people are not finding the kind of spiritual vitality
Jesus described. People desire the simple, powerful, transform=
ing Christianity idealized in the New Testament. Interest in
denominational causes and ecumenism is waning at the grass-
roots. Concern for these matters is centered at the upper eche-
lons, not among the masses. Nor has social action, as the
mission of the church, captured their support. The people are
looking for personal and local church vitality. They are more
like the Greeks who implored, "Sirs, we would see Jesus." The
local church, and more specifically the individual Christian, is
the focal point of the kingdom. That which happens at this
level is ultimately important.

Interest in "good" preaching is increasing. "Good" preaching is the kind of pulpit communication that plugs today's lives
and needs into the power supply of the Word of God.

Much of the new concern and vitality centers in the youth
and young marrieds of the churches. These people are not seeking some "new gospel." In fact, they conservatively affirm the
original values of Christianity. They are not in revolt against
the church, but are dissatisfied with mediocre churches. They
long for the church to become the powerful giant it could be.

The churches that are in trouble are oriented toward preserving human traditions or toward maintaining themselves as institutions, rather than toward accomplishing significant spiritual objectives. People are seeking involvement in meaningful
ministry, and will accept such roles when given adequate
preparation and leadership. But it is increasingly difficult to
rally support for activities in which people see no point. Much
of the current dissatisfaction and disillusionment with churches
grows out of the fact that people perceive much of the activity
as pointless.

The church is a sleeping giant. It has great potential power,
but large portions of its assets are frozen. The church is resil-
ient and tough. It is capable of remarkable recovery. The crisis
of decline has sparked emergency measures and efforts that
had not, until now, been called forth by the legitimate purposes
and objectives of the church. But the important fact is that an
awakening is upon us and the tides are beginning to turn—
whatever the stimulus may have been. We are emerging from
the doldrums of complacency, lethargy, and despair.

This book does not cover many of the details of the life and work of a congregation as a text on church administration would do. Neither does it attempt to present a comprehensive Bible doctrine of the church or church polity. Rather, it focuses upon a philosophy of the church as a foundation for ministry, leadership, and administration. It deals with the purpose of the church, conditions essential to achieving that purpose, factors that tend to obscure or displace that purpose, and solutions to these problems—solutions that are to be found in leadership and planning.

The ideas in this book have been growing for quite some time. I have used and refined them with students in the classroom, with ministers and church staff members in conferences, and with elders, deacons, and other church leaders in retreats and workshops. This book has been written with the hope that it may be of value in the classroom of higher education where Christian leaders are prepared, and in local churches among leaders and members who study, pray, and plan to serve the purposes of Christ as productively as possible.

I am deeply grateful to the authors, colleagues, and the persons mentioned above who have helped stimulate and polish the viewpoint expressed in this book, and to those who have helped to produce this present format.

---

*Leighton Ford, in his Introduction to *The Seven Last Words of the Church* by Ralph Neighbor (Zondervan, 1973), p. 12.

Part One

PURPOSE AS THE KEY

Section Outline

1. *The Power of Purpose*
   A. Purposefulness: What Are We
      Supposed to Be Doing?
   B. Rationality: How Well Are
      We Doing It?

2. *The Nature and Purpose of the Church*
   A. A Philosophy of the Church
   B. The Nature of the Church
   C. The Purpose of the Church

What makes a congregation vigorous and productive? The answer to this question has been elusive. Several factors have been suggested to account for the differences in degree of effectiveness among congregations:

theological position,

location in time and place,

programs and techniques,

variations in the activity of the Holy Spirit or of Satan.

Let's consider these factors.

Doctrinal soundness, while a fundamental necessity, does not by itself guarantee quality of life and high achievement in a congregation. Many churches that would be difficult to fault on their technical orthodoxy are lifeless and unproductive.

Although time and place must be taken into account, this factor alone does not determine the effectiveness of churches. Many congregations have flourished in an unpromising, even hostile, setting; many have failed even in an environment full of opportunity.

What about the third suggested factor? Church leaders have a tendency to seize upon programs and organizational variations found in congregations they consider to be successful. More than likely these adopted elements will fail in already failing churches. The search for the "quick and easy fix" usually leads to efforts that treat symptoms rather than underlying problems.

The fourth suggestion seizes upon some supernatural variation to explain effectiveness or ineffectiveness of churches. Success comes, it is assumed, as God acts more vigorously than usual. The opposition of Satan is used to explain inadequate accomplishment.

God may be considered an always present and always positive factor; Satan, an always present negative factor. Yet the end result fluctuates. Sometimes God's cause moves vigorously ahead, at other times it is static, and at still other times it seems to regress. This fluctuation may be accounted for if the *human element* is seen as the major variable, for God has determined that human beings shall be active agents in these spiritual dynamics. The influence of God or Satan may be augmented or diminished, depending upon the interaction of the human variable. As conditions that are under human control change, the outcome varies.

The major premise of this book is that commitment to purpose is the key to a congregation's effectiveness. Effective congregations vary widely in observable matters of style and program. Productive ministers vary just as widely. If one were to copy these elements in order to become more effective, it would be difficult to know which model to select. But behind these differences lies the common characteristic that may be described as purposefulness, intentionality, deliberateness, goal-orientation, or drive.

Assuming a congregation is doctrinally sound, it is effective to the degree that:

it is clear as to its own identity;

its people are committed and equipped to function;

it is welded together in fellowship;

it is divinely energized;

it controls hindering tendencies;

its leadership function is strong;

every effort is marshalled, directed, and coordinated in the intelligent, deliberate, strategic effort to accomplish God's purpose for it.

1

The Power
of Purpose

As you read, think about these questions:
—What is *purposefulness?* How does it relate to persons, organiza-
tions, and especially congregations?
—What is *rationality?* How does it relate to congregations?
—What is the principle of expediency?
—What aspects of your congregation's life and work must always be
kept as they are because of Scriptural mandate? Which ones might
be open to change?

A consultant to businesses and organizations once described
his function as, "Helping the people with whom I work to ask
and rigorously answer two questions:

What are we supposed to be doing?
and,
How well are we doing it?"

If the people in these institutions would constantly deal with
those two questions, he said, they would never need his high-
priced services. When asked how he would consult with a congregation, he said that he would help the people deal with the
same two issues.

The first question deals with *purposefulness*—that is, the
clear and dominant sense of what one is seeking to accomplish.

The second question deals with *rationality*—that is, the intelligent, deliberate, reasoned actions that move effectively toward accomplishing that purpose.

Purposefulness: What Are We Supposed to Be Doing?

A dear friend and highly disciplined servant of Christ raises homing pigeons as a hobby. I understood his attachment to these creatures when, one day, he took me with him to begin training some young homers. He placed the young birds in a sack in the trunk of his car. We drove to a spot about two miles from his home where he stopped and opened the trunk. He brought out the first bird and soothed it in his hands until it adjusted to the light, and then he threw it into the air. The young bird circled over our heads two or three times, then headed directly for home. When it was out of sight, my friend repeated the procedure with the remaining birds, one at a time. Each bird circled, got its bearings, and headed in exactly the same direction toward home. When we arrived back at the house all the birds were awaiting us.

My friend was very like his birds in one respect—he was goal oriented. His life is totally focused on the consistent goal of accomplishing the purposes of Jesus Christ.

Dynamic individuals and vital groups of people have at least one characteristic in common: they know where they are going, they have a plan for getting there, and they work wholeheartedly at the job.

Successful people have a clear, strong sense of purpose, around which they center their whole lives. They have "hitched their wagons to a star" that serves as a compass bearing, giving consistent direction to every thought and effort. Purpose functions as a gyroscope, giving them stability and renewing balance no matter what direction the fortunes of life may turn them. Purpose integrates life into a consistent, harmonious whole. It provides a driving power, a compelling sense of urgency, that generates and marshals energy.

Some psychologists have suggested that a sense of purpose is a fundamental characteristic of man, and is essential to life. Without it man cannot live satisfactorily and, indeed, may cease to live at all; he is not truly man. (An innate sense of purpose-seeking can be seen in children's persistence in demanding to know the "why" of every aspect of life.)

God is purposeful. He moves unerringly toward consistent objectives. And of all living creatures, man is most like God in his ability to set goals and pursue them intelligently. He alone is able to function as a deliberate partner with God. The Biblical view of history is that of intelligent, deliberate movement toward precise goals in the fulfillment of God's purpose.

Jesus' life was completely coherent because of His single-minded pursuit of a precise objective. Even as a boy, He thought it perfectly obvious that He must be about His Father's business.[1] Of His mission He said, "For the Son of Man came to seek and to save what was lost."[2] "My food," He said, "is to do the will of him who sent me and to finish his work."[3] Faced with a king's hostility that threatened to impede accomplishing His goal, He sent word: "Go tell that fox, 'I will drive out demons and heal people today and tomorrow, and on the third day I will reach my goal.' "[4] When His friends' well-meant but mistaken gestures would have hindered Him, He responded: "Out of my sight, Satan! You are a stumbling block to me; you do not have in mind the things of God, but the things of men."[5] On the evening before the crucifixion and in anticipation of it, He prayed to His Father, "I have brought you glory on the earth by completing the work you gave me to do." The following day, on the cross, His final words were "It is finished."[6]

Because of His single minded commitment to a clear purpose, He could fend off every opposition of friend or foe. He could avoid unproductive effort and channel His entire life toward reaching its precise target.

Jesus' followers shared this quality. The apostle Paul's writings show the steeliness of a totally focused life:

> Do you not know that in a race all the runners run, but only one gets the prize? Run in such a way as to get the prize. Everyone who competes in the games goes into strict training. They do it to get a crown that will not last; but we do it to get a crown that will last forever. Therefore I do not run like a man running aimlessly; I do not fight like a man beating the air.[7]

> Not that I have already obtained all this, or have already been made perfect, but I press on to take hold of that for which Christ Jesus took hold of me. Brothers, I do not consider myself yet to have taken hold of it. But one thing I do: Forgetting what is behind and

straining toward what is ahead, I press on toward the goal to win the prize for which God has called me heavenward in Christ Jesus. All of us who are mature should take such a view of things.[8]

Just as individuals do, vigorous organizations work toward a clearly understood purpose. A clear sense of purpose captivates and rallies the people, welds them together, moves them harmoniously in the same direction, and guides their actions.

The effective church is a body of people who have been "laid hold on" by one mastering, divine purpose. It is captivated by Christ's mission. *His* purpose functions as *its* purpose. Such a church has all the hallmarks of a vigorous organization.

The apostle Paul sought to engender this quality in the congregation at Philippi:

Whatever happens, conduct yourselves in a manner worthy of the gospel of Christ. Then, whether I come and see you or only hear about you in my absence, I will know that you stand firm in one spirit, contending as one man for the faith of the gospel without being frightened in any way by those who oppose you. This is a sign to them that they will be destroyed, but that you will be saved—and that by God. For it has been granted to you on behalf of Christ not only to believe on him, but also to suffer for him, since you are going through the same struggle you saw I had, and now hear that I still have. If you have any encouragement from being united with Christ, if any comfort from his love, if any fellowship with the Spirit, if any tenderness and compassion, then make my joy complete by being like-minded, having the same love, being one in spirit and purpose.[9]

A few years ago Dean M. Kelly sought the reason conservative churches were growing, in contrast to the decline of mainline liberal churches. He found the answer in the level of commitment of the individual church members:

These little bands of committed men and women have an impact on history out of all proportion to their numbers or apparent abilities. In the main, they are usually recruited from the least promising ranks of society; they are not noble or wealthy or well educated or particularly talented. All they have to offer is themselves, but that is more than others give to anything. For when a handful of wholly committed human beings give themselves fully to a great cause or faith, they are virtually irresistible. They cut through the partial fleeting commitments of the rest of society like a buzz saw through peanut brittle.[10]

Power and growth, he concluded, depend upon the ability of a church to mobilize persons around a well-defined central purpose. Conservative churches do that in a way that liberal churches do not.

The effective congregation has a high sense of mission. It is in the world as an alien community and as a task force with a God-given objective. This objective dominates, directs, and drives such a church, to the extent that it is likely to be considered radical by the world (and by innocuous churches). It refuses to accept the role accorded to it by its culture, to accommodate to a less virile image.

Rationality: How Well Are We Doing It?

The effective congregation holds a clear, authentic purpose in common commitment among its members. It also pursues that purpose through a well-reasoned strategy. Its activities or programs are related to its purpose through a carefully worked out rationale. Purpose functions as the touchstone for every thought, decision, plan, or action, and it provides the overall perspective from which each of these can be viewed. If asked about a specific detail of the church's life or program, the members of such a congregation are able to respond, "We do it this way because . . ." and then clearly relate that detail to one or more of the following:

winning people to Christ;

helping Christians incorporate into their lives the details of the Christian way;

helping the congregation to function as the body of Christ;

equipping Christians to perform as God's agents in the world where they live, work and interact in society.

The purposes of God have determined the nature of the church. This, in turn, directs forms and functions—some of which are stipulated by God, and others left to a congregation's discretion. Some aspects of the church are timeless; others are timely.

The core of Biblical "givens" is timeless and unchanging. These matters are stipulated because they are always consistent with, and productive of, the divine purpose. The church's task is to carry them out in a purposeful way, never allowing them to become meaningless routines. These timeless aspects include:

the church as a community of faith, committed to Jesus as Christ and Lord;

a community in which the Bible as God's Word is the rule of faith and practice;

a community existing to reconcile men to God through the gospel, and to nurture Christians in growth toward God's intentions for their lives;

a community overseen and led by elders, served by deacons;

a community practicing baptism as response to the gospel and the Lord's Supper as maintenance of the oath;

a community united on essentials, tolerant in areas of individual freedom, welded together in love.

Timely aspects of the church are those many details of life and work that are left open so that the church may carry out its mission in ways appropriate and effective for its setting. These multitudinous details include: time, place, order, and style of meetings; special plans and programs; type of buildings; and organization of the congregation beyond those matters stipulated for elders and deacons. In such discretionary matters, the church must use the most productive appropriate means at any given moment and place.

Effective congregations are tough-minded in evaluating their efforts and clear-eyed in deciding what to do. They are more concerned with what is *effective* than what they as individuals may *prefer*. They are marked by a willingness to do whatever is necessary, no matter what the cost. In the lives of the individual members, their constant commitment to God's purpose directs their attitudes, motives, thoughts, concerns, lifestyles, behaviors, and temperaments. In congregational concerns, commitment to that purpose is the primary consideration for every ambition, plan, decision, and vote. The degree to which the purpose is being accomplished is never far from the minds of the people.

Take, for example, the question of music styles to be used in the worship services of a congregation. Selection of music is often done by individual preference, rather than rational evaluation and decision. "What I like" is often the emotionally generated standard by which people seek to determine what is used. Sometimes the selection is dictated by traditional assumptions about what is appropriate. A well-reasoned approach asks: (1) What is the role of music in pursuit of the purpose of the church and consistent with the nature of the church; and (2) Which style and selection will fulfill the role best in this time and place?

Each member must be motivated by realizing that his every effort, no matter how small or remote, comes down through a branching system that converges with every other effort to accomplish the master purpose God has ordained. Take, for example, a Christian mother baking cookies for vacation Bible school. It may be difficult to see such an activity as significant to the accomplishing of high goals, and she might approach this task reluctantly, even resentfully, seeing it only as a duty someone persuaded her to do. But if she has a purposeful point of view, she can do it with joy, perceiving it as:

an opportunity to express a personal Christian attitude of loving service,

a means of fulfilling one of her gifts for the body of Christ,

a deliberate contribution to an event where young people will be taught, encouraged in the Lord, and perhaps won to Christ.

In the latter case the woman perceives her efforts as one tributary merging with many others to form an enlarging stream that accomplishes significant goals. This ability to view one's actions from a larger perspective is the key to healthy motivation of Christians.

Paul demonstrates the characteristic of Christian rationality. For example, which is better—to be in want and privation or to have plenty? Paul would welcome whichever condition might best serve the interests of Christ. Is it preferable to be free or in prison? If his freedom would serve Christ, he would defend and use it; if prison were to be his lot, he would seek to make even that productive of Christ's interests. Is it preferable to live or die? Again, the primary consideration is, *Which would be more productive for Christ?* Paul considered himself dead to self-interest and to the usual values of the world. Since Christ is Lord, Paul and all the conditions of his life were yielded to His service. Fulfilling Christ's purpose was the overwhelming concern against which he weighed every other consideration.[11]

In the same way the effective congregation weighs every decision and evaluates every consideration in light of how it contributes to accomplishing Christ's mission. This is the grand obsession of all Christians, individually and collectively as the church. With this kind of mentality, the church is pro-active, rather than reactive; it pursues goals, rather than responding to emerging pressures; it is intentional, rather than reflexive; it functions by design, rather than by accident or whim.

The difference between a swamp and a millrace illustrates the effect of purposefulness. A relatively small quantity of water can set in motion a large waterwheel which, in turn, powers machinery so that work is accomplished. The secret is in the narrow channeling of the water and the precision with which it strikes the wheel. A swamp, on the other hand, may contain a vast quantity of water that never accomplishes anything because it is directionless—aimless, inert, and stagnant.

Effective congregations tend to resemble the millrace; ineffective ones, the swamp.

Purpose is the target that provides order and gives meaning to the church. If an objective is broad and general, many different efforts will seem equally appropriate for achieving it. But if the objective is defined specifically, it is obvious which of the prospective efforts will strike it most centrally and, therefore, which is preferable. In practice, however, purpose is often assumed and left unstated, or it may be couched in vague generalities. If the church lacks a sharp focus upon its target, it will drift aimlessly through a maze of activities, toward no discernible destination. The clever and yet profound bit of wisdom says, "If you don't know where you are going, one direction is as good as another."

A caution is in order here against what has been called "the cult of the new"—the assumption that different is always better. Ineffective new ways are no better than ineffective old ways. The criterion for the methods a church uses is *effectiveness in accomplishing the church's purpose*—not whether a method is old or new, traditional or innovative.

Often church leaders must choose between reinvesting an existing practice with meaning so that it is productive of purpose, or introducing a new way to achieve the purpose. Given such a choice, the first option may be preferable since it requires only one task: communicating purpose. The second option makes two demands upon the leaders: communicating purpose and "selling" people on a new way (an undertaking that may compound the problem).

Summary

In this chapter, two characteristics of an effective congregation have been discussed: purposefulness and rationality. *Purposefulness* deals with focusing upon clear, authentic goals; *rationality,* with reaching those goals through effective methods.

For Further Reading

Benjamin, Paul. *The Growing Congregation.* Cincinnati: Standard Publishing, 1975.
Getz, Gene. *Sharpening the Focus of the Church.* Chicago: Moody Press, 1974.
————. *The Measure of a Church.* Glendale: Regal, 1975.
Kelly, Dean. *Why Conservative Churches Are Growing.* New York: Harper and Row, 1972.
McGavran, Donald A. and Arn, Winfield. *Ten Steps for Church Growth.* New York: Harper and Row, 1977.
Perry, Lloyd. *Getting the Church on Target.* Chicago: Moody Press, 1977.
Richards, Larry. *A New Face for the Church.* Grand Rapids: Zondervan, 1970.
Saucy, Robert L. *The Church in God's Program.* Northbrook, IL: Moody Press, 1972.
Snyder, Howard A. *The Community of the King.* Downers Grove, IL: Inter-Varsity Press, 1977.
Stedman, Ray. *Authentic Christianity.* Waco, TX: Word, 1975.
Tippett, Alan. *Church Growth and the Word of God.* Grand Rapids: Eerdmans, 1970.

---

[1]Luke 2:49
[2]Luke 19:10
[3]John 4:34
[4]Luke 13:32
[5]Matthew 16:23
[6]John 17:4; 19:30
[7]1 Corinthians 9:24-26
[8]Philippians 3:12-15
[9]Philippians 1:27—2:2
[10]Dean M. Kelly, *Why Conservative Churches Are Growing.* (New York: Harper and Row, 1972), p. 51.
[11]Philippians 1:20-26

2

The Nature and Purpose of the Church

As you read, think about these questions:
—What is meant by a "philosophy of the church"?
—How would you define the church? What is its nature? Its purpose?
—What is the relationship between evangelism and Christian nurture?
—How clear is your congregation's self-image and its understanding of its purpose?

A Philosophy of the Church

Everyone has a philosophy according to which he thinks and acts. It may be consistent or filled with contradictions, true or false, clear or muddled. It may be held consciously or unconsciously. A person's philosophy is his conceptual map of the nature and purpose of things, how things ought to be, and how things really are; a schematic of views, premises, assumptions, and convictions that give him direction. A philosophy is the ground out of which decisions and practices grow. It is the standard by which ideas are tested, the compass by which to plan and move ahead.

Actions grow out of our *operating* value system—that is, what we *really* believe; our deepest convictions. It is dangerously easy to espouse one philosophy and operate by another. Sometimes we must reason backward from practice to identify the actual philosophy in operation. For example, the church may verbalize a Biblically ideal philosophy, but *operate* out of a philosophy of institutional expedience. Effectiveness requires an integrity in which practice conforms to ideals.

Adequate and inadequate philosophies can be contrasted as follows:

Adequate	*Inadequate*
Explicit	Implicit
Gives rise to cohesive, consistent thought and action	Gives rise to random, contradictory thought and action
We employ it	We are at its mercy
Behavior is likely to be deliberate, intentional, rational, productive	Behavior is likely to be reactive, irrational, unproductive

If a congregation is to reach a high level of effective life and achievement, its members and its leaders must arrive at a consistent, clear, and accurate philosophy that is held in common and that guides the corporate effort. The people must be clear and unified on such questions as:

What are we (that is, the church)?
Why are we here?
Where are we going?
How can we get from here to there?
How should we function?

These are precisely the elements the apostle Paul fervently desired the church in Colosse to possess:

For this reason, since the day we heard about you, we have not stopped praying for you and asking God to fill you with the knowledge of his will through all spiritual wisdom and understanding. And we pray this in order that you may live a life worthy of the Lord and may please him in every way: bearing fruit in every good work, growing in the knowledge of God, being strengthened with all power according to his glorious might so that you may have great endurance and patience, and joyfully giving thanks to the Father, who has qualified you to share in the inheritance of the saints in the kingdom of light. For he has rescued us from the dominion of darkness and brought us into the kingdom of the Son he loves, in whom we have redemption, the forgiveness of sins.[1]

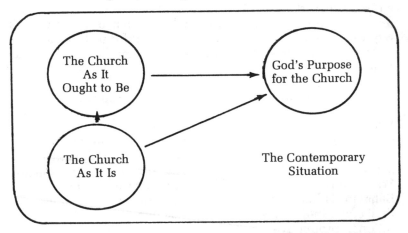

Congregations must seek a clear understanding of the following elements: God's purpose for the church, the church as it is intended to be, the church as it actually is, and the contemporary situation in which it functions as it pursues its purpose.

The leaders of a congregation must help "what is" move toward conformity to "what ought to be." They must help the church understand and effectively engage its given time and place in fulfilling God's purposes.

The Nature of the Church[2]

What is this entity called the church? A description of its nature can best be approached through a Biblical world view.

Creation and Re-creation

God created human life, designing it to function according to certain principles and to occupy certain relationships with the material creation, with other human lives, and with himself.

God intended that He and man maintain a voluntary, free, open, collaborative relationship. He desired that man's response to Him be one of freely chosen, intelligent trust and obedience. As created and when operating according to intention, life was pronounced "good." It worked; it functioned according to design; it was in harmony with reality (Genesis 1, 2).

However, Satan engaged God in a titanic struggle for man's allegiance. He opposed God's intentions with contrary purposes, values, and principles for living. He proposed for people a contrary set of relationships with the material creation and with each other. He sought to engage man in a relationship of subtlety, manipulation, deception, and bondage (Genesis 3).

The first man elected Satan's alternatives, and his life deflected from God's intention. His life was thrown out of order as it deviated from the way it was designed to work. It entered into a state of tension and discord with the principles structured into creation itself.

The result of the first man's sin was alienation from God, guilt, disharmony with reality, confused values and purposes, frustrated labor, pain, and death. Even the rest of creation was thrown off course in the process (Genesis 3:17, 18; Romans 8:19-22). Satan became, for the time being, prince of this world (John 12:31, 14:30).

Since that time, human beings by birth have become partakers of the physical distortion that includes disease and death (Romans 5:12-14). We also enter the present world's sociological and psychological disorder. As we choose Satan's counterprinciples for life, which are deeply ingrained in the world's values and ways (Romans 6:23; Galatians 3:22), we become partakers of spiritual distortion—sin—and the resulting alienation from God. Knowing how God intended life to be, Jesus looked upon the human scene with a profound sense of tragedy (Matthew 9:36).

From the beginning, however, God planned to restore all things to His originally intended state without violating His own principles for interacting with man (Ephesians 1:3-14; 3:9-12; Acts 3:21). Paul refers to this plan of God as the mystery or secret, hidden to all generations of the human race until fully revealed in Jesus (Colossians 1:26, 27).

Jesus, as the second Adam (1 Corinthians 15:45), entered the now-alien kingdom of the world. Through Him re-creation began, whereby lives can be restored to the creation design (2 Corinthians 5:17; Galatians 6:15). The purpose of God in Jesus was to redeem man, not condemn him, and reestablish life as intended (John 3:14-21; 1:4, 5; 14:6). Jesus, the Redeemer, gave His life as a sacrifice to reconcile man to God and to remove the condemnation of sin (2 Corinthians 5:19; Colossians 1:20; Romans 5:6, 12-19; 6:22, 23; 1 Timothy 1:15; 1 Peter 3:18).

Through Him man is inducted into the grace of God and thus restored to the intended relationship with God (Ephesians 3:19). His resurrection authenticated this function and established Him as Lord.

Jesus also reintroduced God's purposes, values, and principles of conduct for life (2 Timothy 1:9; Colossians 3:1—4:6). He not only revealed the way life was designed to work; He provided a perfect living demonstration. Through committing themselves to Jesus as their Savior, His followers are reconciled to God. Through committing themselves to Him as Lord, they are introduced into a way of life that is in harmony with principles rooted in the foundations of the world.

The Christian Community

The Christian way of thinking and acting does not match the so-called "natural" patterns of life. It is *super-natural*, revolutionary, radical. But the Christian commits himself to incorporate the details of this way into his life, confident that they are true. He implements the ways Jesus revealed even when they run counter to his inclinations. He distrusts and rejects the world's principles, values, and moral standards, even when they seem preferable.

The Christian believes that the Bible contains precepts he is expected to incorporate into his life. It is not only that these precepts are true because they are in the Bible—they are in the Bible because they are true. The way of Christ is looked upon as the one right way, revealed and to be followed in detail.

Our lives must be in proper adjustment to spiritual reality if they are to be meaningful, if they are to work. In a similar way, a television set receives a picture because a natural law is being utilized. The law is mysterious, but the set works as long as it is in harmony with the law. If the set gets out of adjustment, meaningless confusion results. The natural law is not to blame; the problem is in the television set. The set will work only when it is properly harmonized with that law.

Christianity is God's way of providing that kind of adjustment. As God's principles are incorporated by the Christian, life progressively functions as God intended. Ways of thinking and acting are transformed from "the pattern of this world" to God's "good, pleasing, and perfect will" (Romans 12:2). The person who chooses to follow Christ deliberately leaves the kingdom of Satan for the kingdom of God, "dying" to the for-

mer way in order to live Christ's way (Colossians 1:13; 1 Peter
2:9; Romans 6:1-23). Becoming a Christian is more than reform
or simply *adding* religion to life; it is revolution so complete
that Jesus called it being "born again" (John 3:3), that one
might enter a new kind of existence (2 Corinthians 5:17).

People become followers of Jesus Christ as they consider the
offer posed by the gospel, respond in the stipulated obedience,
and stake everything that God's propositions are true, rejecting
all other alternatives. Collectively, these people are the church,
and have a corporate identity as well as individual identities.

Presently, then, two kingdoms exist in the world: one in
which Satan and his way prevail, the other in which Jesus
Christ is Lord and God's way prevails. This simple two-
category classification is dominant in Jesus' teaching: the two
roads (Matthew 7:13, 14); the wheat and the tares (Matthew
13:24-30); the separation of fish (Matthew 13:47-50); the two
masters (Matthew 6:24).

As the ways of the world move farther and farther from the
intentions of God, as seems to be the present trend, the distinc-
tiveness of Christ's people intensifies. The church is not merely
a variation of the world, but God's kingdom, a colony of
Heaven implanted in the world. Christianity and the world
represent two entirely different systems or orders of life. The
differences are numerous and profound:

The Church	The World
Reconciled	Alienated
Truth	Error
Understanding	Confusion
Citizen with God	Alien to God
Alien to world	Citizen of the world
Hope	Without Hope
Saved	Lost
In light	In darkness
Wholeness	Brokenness
Mind of the Spirit	Mind of flesh, world
Life	Death
Free in Christ	Bondage
Ways of God	Ways of world, Satan
Obedient	Disobedient
Peace with God	Enmity with God

God's restoration of the world into conformity with His intention will be complete (Romans 8:18-21). Satan's alternatives
will be ultimately unmasked, judged, and removed (2 Thessalonians 2:1-12). Only Christ's church will remain—
vindicated and brought to total fulfillment (2 Peter 3:13; 1 Corinthians 15:24; Revelation 20:11—21:8). In the meantime, the
implanted church must grow, permeate the world, and embrace more and more people into this distinct relationship with
God and His way of life (Matthew 13:31-33).

Summary

The church is a distinctive body of people who:

1. Have been reconciled to God through a decisive response
   to Jesus Christ as Savior.
2. Through a commitment to Jesus Christ as Lord, deliberately incorporate into life the ways of thought and conduct revealed by Him as God's design for living. They are
   in the world, but not of the world.
3. Function together in congregations, implementing the intended relationship: love.
4. Aggressively engage the world, seeking to enlist others as
   disciples of Jesus Christ, so that the number of the saved
   increases and the number of the lost diminishes.
5. Anticipate the full and final restoration of all things to
   God's perfect intention.

An early Christian document known as the letter to Diognetus describes Christ's people in this way:

Christians cannot be distinguished from the rest of the human
race by country or language or customs. They do not live in cities of
their own; they do not use a peculiar form of speech; they do not
follow an eccentric manner of life. This doctrine of theirs has not
been discovered by the ingenuity of deep thought of inquisitive
men, nor do they put forward merely human teaching, as some
people do. Yet, although they live in Greek and barbarian cities
alike, as each man's lot has been cast, and follow the customs of the
country in clothing and food and other matters of daily living, at the
same time they give proof of the remarkable and admittedly extraor-
dinary constitution of their own commonwealth. They live in their
own countries, but only as aliens. They have a share in everything as
citizens, and endure everything as foreigners. Every foreign land is
their fatherland, and yet for them every fatherland is a foreign

land. . . . It is true that they are "in the flesh," but they do not live "according to the flesh." They busy themselves on earth, but their citizenship is in heaven. They obey the established laws, but in their own lives they go far beyond what the laws require.[3]

The Purpose of the Church

The purpose of God in the world is evident in the nature of the church: *to reconcile persons to himself and to restore their lives to working order, in harmony with His design.*

The church is both the product of God's purpose and the means for achieving it. The church is divinely energized in order that it may accomplish its God-given purpose; and, conversely, it is divinely energized *to the degree* that it pursues that purpose. The church is to be the community of God's people, thinking and acting as God intended and inviting others, on behalf of God, to join the community. Thus, Paul identified his obsession in life: "We proclaim him, admonishing and teaching everyone with all wisdom, so that we may present everyone perfect in Christ. To this end I labor, struggling with all his energy, which so powerfully works in me."[4]

The *operational* purpose of the church is precisely stated in Jesus' Commission to His people: "All authority in heaven and on earth has been given to me. Therefore go and make disciples of all nations, baptizing them in the name of the Father and of the Son and of the Holy Spirit, and teaching them to obey everything I have commanded you. And surely I will be with you always, to the very end of the age."[5]

The central imperative in the Commission is "make disciples" of all nations or "disciple all the peoples." The other verb forms—*go, baptize, teach,* cluster around "make disciples." Go into all the world—and make disciples. Baptizing them—to make disciples. Further instructing them in the way—as disciples. Simply going into all the world is not fulfilling the Commission; making disciples is.

Purposes such as social improvement are by-products of the church's operational purpose, and are accomplished indirectly. The law of indirection states that some goals (happiness, for example) cannot be directly achieved, but can be achieved only as other related goals are accomplished. Some of the purposes of the church are this way also, and can be achieved only in the process of fulfilling the central purpose.

God may have transcendent purposes that we may or may not perceive. Some would insist, for example, that the purpose of the church is to bring glory to God. That may be true, but *operationally*, how does one bring glory to God? By fulfilling the purpose defined above. Jesus said to His Father, "I have brought you glory on earth by completing the work you gave me to do."[6] Whatever transcendent purposes God may have, they are accomplished by faithful carrying out of the tasks He has assigned.

Evangelism and Nurture

The operational purpose of the church is to bring the people of the world into discipleship to Jesus. This is carried out in the twin processes of evangelism and nurture. These processes, like head and tail of a coin, cannot be split apart and remain a whole Commission. They may be compared and described in the following way:

Evangelism	*Nurture*
1. Directed toward the unsaved	1. Directed toward Christians
2. Salvation	2. Growth
3. Reconciles man to God	3. Reconciles man's ways to God's ways
4. Restores relationship and capability	4. Restores function
5. Inducts individuals into the community of God's people	5. Edifies individuals toward maturity or full functioning in terms of the norms of God's people
6. Initial function	6. Continuing function
7. Recruits followers	7. Equips followers to live and serve
8. Birth	8. Growth
9. Quantitative growth of the church	9. Qualitative growth of the church
10. Carried out by all Christians	10. Carried out by all Christians
11. Takes place wherever Christians contact the un-	11. Takes place wherever Christians are in con-

saved, but primarily in the world

tact, but especially in the fellowship of the church

12. Uses contacts for witnessing, preaching the gospel, and teaching

12. Uses fellowship, teaching the Word, and training in needed skills

13. Objective is that people accept Christ as Savior and Lord.

13. Objectives are: (a) to help Christians live Christ's way more fully; (b) to help them find and develop their gifts so they may function fully within the church; (c) to provide for growth and training so that each member may be equipped for his role in the world

14. Carries promise of divine presence

14. Carries promise of divine presence

15. Empowered by the Holy Spirit

15. Empowered by the Holy Spirit

The often-expressed disagreements over qualitative versus quantitative growth of the church are the result of failure to perceive both functions as a whole purpose. Each function is inadequate if it does not contribute to the other. Evangelism provides the disciples and sets the stage for their nurture; nurture equips disciples so that evangelism is further expanded. Evangelism that does not lead to nurture for growth is inadequate. Likewise, nurture that does not provide for Christian effectiveness that enhances evangelism is also inadequate. The goal is more and better Christians in more, better, and bigger congregations until the peoples of the world have become the people of Christ.

The process may be pictured this way:

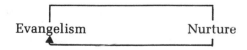

Evangelism   Nurture

Evangelism must carry over into the nurture of those who are recruited to follow Christ, and nurture must encompass at least three aspects of life:

1. *Personal Christian living.* Nurture provides for the transformation of the details of thought and action into the revolutionary lifestyle that characterizes the followers of Jesus. To this world, the Christian is an alien life-form, born of the Spirit, born from above, and a partaker of the divine nature. He must be assisted to change from living as the "natural man" to living as the "spiritual man." As a baby must learn all about life in the world, so the person who has undergone new birth into the kingdom must learn this new way of living.

Progressively, the Christian's personal life is brought into conformity to God's design. This includes his devotional relationship with God, thought patterns, motives, ambitions, values, morals, ethics, attitudes, goals, and personal and family conduct.

The purposeful Christian pursues personal growth—not as a grim duty or dull routine, but as an exciting adventure as he continues to discover the glory of God's design for the abundant life.[7] He is intent on making progress toward the goal of total Christlikeness. The purposeful congregation carefully and deliberately provides means for helping Christians grow in the adventure of Christian living.

As this transformation occurs, further evangelism follows naturally. The Christian influences non-Christians by encountering them with a life restored to God's design.[8] This reinforcing cycle may be pictured in this way:

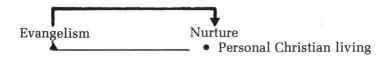

Evangelism   Nurture
                         • Personal Christian living

2. *Functioning in the body of Christ.* Nurture also enables Christians to fit harmoniously and productively into the Christian community—the church. The church is a fellowship of people functioning together in harmony and treating one another as God intended people to do. This is a restored social condition, a working model of the heavenly relationship, and a foretaste of the ultimate state the redeemed will enjoy in eter-

nity. Each individual must seriously apply himself to discovering, developing, and using his abilities or talents for building up the body of Christ. And he must be aided in doing so by the specific efforts of his congregation. This attitude of mutual helpfulness not only helps the church to function better, but it shows non-Christians the intentions of God demonstrated in the love Christians have for one another. Thus the cycle continues to expand:

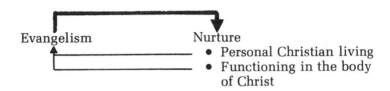

Evangelism   Nurture
                                • Personal Christian living
                                • Functioning in the body
                                  of Christ

3. *Functioning in the world.* Finally, nurture equips Christians to live deliberately as God's people in the world. This aspect of the purpose is concerned with how the Christian's commitment works out in his roles of employer, employee, citizen, neighbor, friend. A large proportion of the letters to Christians in the New Testament deals with the practical details of their relationships with others.[9] This element of nurture also augments evangelism in the following ways:

indirectly, through the positive influence of these contacts on non-Christians;

informally, as Christians seek to communicate their faith when occasions arise;

formally, as Christians specifically approach non-Christians with a view to persuading them to become followers of Jesus.

Once again the cycle expands:

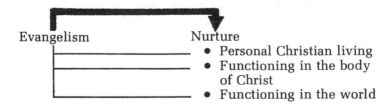

Evangelism   Nurture
                                • Personal Christian living
                                • Functioning in the body
                                  of Christ
                                • Functioning in the world

Conversion and nurture form a powerful spiral of mutually reinforcing cycles, in which Jesus' purpose of discipling the nations is accomplished. The book of Acts first records that people were "added" to the church. As the tornado-like process began to generate power, the record notes that believers "multiplied." The possibilities of exponential growth of the church stagger the imagination. It is little wonder that a Christian writer in the second century could remark that Christians had so increased in number that they constituted "all but a majority in every city."

For Further Reading

Getz, Gene. *Sharpening the Focus of the Church*. Chicago: Moody Press, 1974.
_____. *The Measure of a Church*. Glendale: Regal, 1975.
Griffith, Leonard. *God and His People*. Nashville: Abingdon, 1960.
MacArthur, John. *The Church, The Body of Christ*. Grand Rapids: Zondervan, 1973.
Miller, Donald G. *The Nature and Mission of the Church*. Oak Park, Illinois: John Knox Press, 1957.
Minear, Paul S. *Images of the Church in the New Testament*. Philadelphia: Westminster Press, 1965.
Saucy, Robert L. *The Church in God's Program*. Northbrook, Illinois: Moody Press, 1972.
Stedman, Ray. *Body Life*. Ventura, California: Regal, 1972.
Tippett, Alan. *Church Growth and the Word of God*. Grand Rapids: Eerdmans, 1970.

---

[1]Colossians 1:9-14
[2]Since this section specifically presents the Biblical picture of the nature of the church, Scripture references will remain in the text. Otherwise, Scripture references will be footnoted as all other references are.
[3]Letter to Diognetus, 5:1-10. *Early Christian Fathers,* translated and edited by Cyril C. Richardson, *The Library of Christian Classics,* Volume I. Philadelphia: The Westminster Press, 1953.
[4]Colossians 1:28, 29
[5]Matthew 28:18-20
[6]John 17:4
[7]2 Corinthians 3:18; Philippians 2:12, 13
[8]1 Peter 2:12; 1 Thessalonians 4:11, 12
[9]See, for example, Romans 12:14—13:14

Part Two

ESSENTIAL CONDITIONS FOR ACCOMPLISHING THE PURPOSE

Section Outline

3. *Committed People*
   - A. Co-laborers With God
   - B. Commitment and Discipleship
   - C. Key to the Success of the Church

4. *Equipping the People*
   - A. The Equipping Model
   - B. An Equipping Ministry
   - C. An Equipping Structure
   - D. An Equipping Program

5. *Fellowship*
   - A. The Uniqueness of Christian Fellowship
   - B. Fellowship and Purpose
   - C. Developing Fellowship in the Church

6. *Spiritual Power*
   - A. Divine Resources Required
   - B. Purpose and Power
   - C. The Current Scene
   - D. How Congregations Can Regain Spiritual Power

Some Christian leaders frantically search for an elusive key that will unlock the secrets of congregational vitality. Many become frustrated over the inertia, unproductivity, and unwillingness of churches. Ministers, in particular, are often frustrated at their inability to cope with the conditions they face in their congregations.

The good news for churches and their leaders is this: Radically new forms, structures, programs, or personnel are not required for churches to become more effective. The solution is less complicated than often assumed. The difference between a moribund congregation and a vital one is not necessarily vast. Moving from a static to a vigorous condition does not usually require a revolution. The answer often lies in a simple shift of orientation toward purpose.

Evangelism and nurture were described in the last chapter as reciprocating processes. Each augments the other in a powerful cycle. A similar relationship exists between a set of specific conditions and the purpose of the church. This section deals with four such conditions: committed people, equipped people, fellowship, and spiritual power. These four conditions contribute to accomplishing God's purpose for the church, and they also are augmented as God's purpose is accomplished. A purposeful orientation on the part of the church and its leaders

41

sets in motion dynamic cycles involving each of these conditions.

The effect of such a reorientation toward purpose can be illustrated by the surveying of land. If a surveyor shifts direction only slightly at one point, enormous difference results down the line. The farther one goes, the bigger the difference becomes.

Developing a purposeful orientation sometimes requires only a subtle sharpening of focus, a recasting of attitude, so that existing forms take a fresh meaning and productivity. The church can infuse its people with a sense of partnership with God if it marshalls the details of its life and program in such a way that every function and event becomes intentional, directional, and significant.

CHAPTER

3

Committed People: The Basic Unit of Responsibility

As you read, think about these questions:
—What is the relationship between salvation and commitment in the life of a Christian?
—Why is Christian faithfulness more than a matter of simple stead-fastness, or of surviving to the end of a life without repudiating Christ?
—Is the concept of individual commitment and responsibility unique to Christianity?
—How would you analyze your congregation in terms of the ideals and problems discussed in this chapter?

The church is the product of God's purpose and, at the same time, the instrument by which that purpose is furthered. It consists of people who are restored to the proper relationship with God and who are being restored to life as God designed it. The church is also the means by which other people are brought into this restored relationship. The church exists to grow, both in size and in quality.

God's purpose must also be the purpose of each person in the church. Ultimately, the functional unit must be the individual Christian who:

progressively and deliberately incorporates the details of
the Christian way into his life,

uses whatever gifts he has to help himself to mature and
the corporate church to grow and build itself up in love,

works out the implications of salvation in his interactions
in the world, including the recruiting of others to become
disciples of Jesus.

Accomplishment of the goals of Christianity must be the
focal point of commitment for both congregation and individuals.

The church consists of Christians collaborating to help one
another fulfill these objectives, individually and in concert.

Co-laborers With God

God has consistently pursued His objectives in this world
through people: through individuals such as Abraham, or
through people in groups such as the nation of Israel. In this
final epoch in His plan—the Christian era—God works through
the followers of Jesus Christ. This body of people—of many
peoples, tongues, and races—are His indispensible partners in
the task. As from the beginning, God preserves the integrity of
His people, respects their freedom of will, and honors their
rights to initiative. He allows them awesome control over the
status and progress of His cause.

Let's compare two occasions on which God's people stood on
the brink of the future. In the first instance, God's program
suffered a severe reverse because of the people. In the second,
committed people accomplished great things for (and with)
their Lord.

The nation that had grown out of Abraham's family stood at
the border of a land God had promised them. By a series of
spectacular miracles God had liberated these people from
Egyptian slavery. He had parted the waters of the Red Sea before them. He had led this liberated throng through the wilderness, providing water when they were thirsty and food when
they were hungry. At Sinai He had given them the details for
living and functioning as His people, and set forth a complete
religious-social arrangement for this nation. Soon the people
stood at the border of the land God promised them. It was here,

God promised, that they and He would work together to accomplish His purposes for the world.

God told them He would give them the land; they were to go in and possess it. Instead, the people made camp at the border while a dozen men went through the land on a reconnaissance mission. Upon their return, the men unanimously appraised the land as a desirable place; it flowed with milk and honey. But the majority of the men said it could never be theirs. It was already inhabited, and the inhabitants were gigantic and armed, and they lived in fortified cities. "We seemed like grasshoppers in our own eyes," the spies said, "and we looked the same to them."[1] Only two of the twelve men appealed for confidence in the promises of God to go forward.

The people collapsed in despair. At the brink of attainment, they failed God and themselves. They turned back to the wilderness, where for four decades they camped as wanderers, until all that unprofitable adult generation—except for the two faithful men—died and were replaced by a new generation with whom God could better work. God's purpose and plans were set back a whole generation through no fault of His own, but solely because of the people.

The occasion was strikingly different when Jesus commissioned His followers. They were a little band of nobodies in the opinion of the world: nobodies compared to the power and wealth of Rome; nobodies compared to the sophistication of Greece; nobodies compared to the religious establishment in Jerusalem. Eleven men formed a more intimate cadre; some 120 people comprised the larger following. But they wore people who had seen and heard Jesus, witnessed His death, and met with Him after His resurrection. They were convinced this Jesus was God's Son, the Messiah, and they had committed themselves to Him and to His cause. Now He commissioned them to make all the peoples of the world His disciples. They were nobodies and there were giants in the land, but on Pentecost they began to move, to implement the commission.

Consider what God had done for these people. Centuries of patient preparation had culminated in God's sending of His Son—the longed-for Savior, Redeemer, Messiah—into the world. Jesus had given His life to save these people from ruin and restore them to fellowship with God. He had purchased this new community, the church, with His own blood. And,

wonder of all wonders, God had raised Him from the dead,
declaring Him with power to be the Son of God. In addition,
God poured His Spirit upon His people, to be their divine col-
laborator and enabler for their task of making disciples of all
the world.

Christians were awestruck by the wonderful thing that had
happened to them. They had been formed into a kingdom of
priests, a holy nation, to serve God. They were stewards of
divine truth and grace. Theirs was the astonishing privilege of
implementing the very plans of God! Christianity stood in stark
and thrilling contrast to life as they had known it before. The
hopelessness and despair of their former condition were still
vivid. God's love, grace, and salvation had made a staggering
impact upon them.

Their objectives and responsibilities as Christians were fresh
and compelling. They had an aching concern for those who
still lacked the precious gift of Christ, a concern born of the
glad wonder of salvation and the intense presence of Christ in
their own lives. As long as there was one person who had not
shared in this wonderful treasure, they could not rest.

Their numbers grew and multiplied. The world reeled at
their impact. God's purposes moved forward in a breathtaking
way. What happened in the next few decades would be too
fantastic to believe if it were not a matter of history.

Commitment and Discipleship

The same gospel that calls us to salvation also calls us to
commitment in promoting the cause of Christ as first priority in
life. Humanly devised religions typically are efforts of man to
get God on his side; man seeks to persuade God to join him in
order to accomplish what he wants. In Christianity, however,
man joins God to serve His purposes. In the one, man seeks to
use God; in the other, man seeks to be used by God.

When one becomes a disciple, he receives salvation and is
recruited into Christ's task force. He cannot choose the gift of
God without accepting the attendant commitment any more
than he could pick up one side of a coin without the other.
Findley Edge illustrates this point:

> One friend meets another and says, "There is something impor-
> tant going on down at Fourth and Broadway. Come and share it with

me." The second friend says, "Thanks, I'll be delighted to accept your invitation." The second person knows that there is a large hotel at Fourth and Broadway, and he has heard that they are having a banquet there with excellent food and entertainment. When they arrive, however, an Army recruitment booth has been set up in front of the hotel, and his friend wants him to enlist for war. The second friend could only plead, "Excuse me! I didn't know this was what you had in mind!" He had responded to the "banquet" idea but not to the army. Thus, his initial commitment or response, regardless of how sincere and genuine it may have been when he made it, was not sound because that to which he had committed himself was different from that to which he was invited.

This homely example may not be too far off, at that. Some respond to the invitation of God as though He was inviting them to a feast, an eternal party in Heaven, when in reality He is inviting them to enlist for war.[2]

The gospel invites us to both the spiritual banquet and the army.[3] But attention must be directed to the militancy of discipleship because Christians are so prone to neglect it, as Elton Trueblood has observed:

> One of the most surprising facts about the early Church was its fundamental similarity to a military band. . . . The notion of enlisting Church members as recruits sounds very strange to modern ears. This reaction tells us something significant about the Church of the twentieth century; it tells us how far we have drifted.[4]

Sacrament is not a Biblical term, but it did appear quite early in Christianity. Hans-Reudi Weber suggests a highly plausible explanation for the adoption of the term.[5] The church was born in a world dominated by the Roman Empire. In those days it was the ambition of nearly every young man to become a soldier in the legions of Caesar. When a man was accepted, he entered the military through a life-changing oath, in which he forfeited all other allegiances and loyalties. He committed himself without reservation to Caesar and his cause. His time, fortunes, concerns, and life itself belonged to his king. He would live for him, labor for him, fight for him, and die for him. He no longer had any claim on himself; His emperor and the empire would be his reason for living from that moment forward. Nothing was reserved or held back. The solemn oath by which a man ceased being a civilian and committed himself to his king was, in the Latin language, the *sacramentum*.

It is not difficult to see how those early Christians would draw a parallel to this military practice. They could well have said, "We, too, have an emperor: Jesus Christ, King of kings and Lord of lords. We are as fully committed to Him as any soldier ever could be to a human emperor. We, too, have taken the oath, the *sacramentum*. In our baptism, we became completely His." Thus, baptism came to be described as the Christian sacrament or oath.

Weber further suggests that the term *pagan* meant, among other things, a civilian, one who is not a soldier. Therefore one was either Christ's soldier or a pagan (civilian).

It would have been an obvious next step for those early Christian soldiers of Christ to realize that their oath to Him was reaffirmed week after week in the Lord's Supper. Thus it, too, came to be called a Christian sacrament.

The irony about today's church membership, according to Weber, is that so many who have apparently joined Christ's army never engage in the struggle for the world. Many desert the cause entirely; others take a permanent leave; still others always remain recruits, practicing their use of the spiritual armor, but never venturing out on the battlefield. "Under these circumstances," muses Weber, "no wonder the battle soon begins in the barracks!"[6]

Christ's Teachings

This kind of radical commitment is mandatory for a true disciple of Jesus Christ. Jesus himself spelled out, in no uncertain terms, the degree of commitment He required. He insisted upon a clear-eyed, deliberate choice to become one of His followers:

> The kingdom of heaven is like a treasure hidden in a field. When a man found it, he hid it again, and then in his joy went and sold all he had and bought that field. Again, the kingdom of heaven is like a merchant looking for fine pearls. When he found one of great value, he went away and sold everything he had and bought it.[7]

> If anyone would come after me, he must deny himself and take up his cross and follow me.[8]

> If anyone comes to me and does not hate his father and mother, his wife and children, his brothers and sisters—yes, even his own life—he cannot be my disciple. And anyone who does not carry his

cross and follow me cannot be my disciple. . . . Any of you who does not give up everything he has cannot be my disciple.[9]

In this last passage, a difficult one, Jesus is talking about attitudes and values rather than about literal behavior. However, the impact is unmistakable: the terms for being one of Jesus' people include total commitment. Jesus' followers must "sell out" to Him. They must deny themselves. Nothing can take priority over their commitment to Him.

Jesus called for such a decisive verdict from the twelve. They had been with Him for some time; they had watched His deeds, heard His words, weighed their conclusions. Then at Caesarea Philippi, He questioned them about public opinion regarding his identity. After they had listed the various opinions, He pressed for their conclusion. Simon Peter answered for them, "You are the Christ, the Son of the living God."[10] These men later staked everything on that conclusion in such a way that their lives were dominated and directed—even to martyrdom—by it. A later addition to their number, Paul, shared their decisive commitment. As he compared his life and values before obedience to Christ with his life and values as Christ's follower, he wrote,

> But whatever was to my profit I now consider loss for the sake of Christ. What is more, I consider everything a loss compared to the surpassing greatness of knowing Christ Jesus my Lord, for whose sake I have lost all things. I consider them rubbish, that I may gain Christ and be found in him. . . .[11]

The level of commitment of the apostles can be seen in their prayers, recorded in the book of Acts. They encountered severe opposition. Their leaders had been arrested and commanded to cease their efforts—commanded by the same authorities that had been able to bring Jesus to crucifixion not long before. When the church gathered, however, their prayers were not for their own safety but for the success of the Lord's cause.[12] They were expendable, the cause was not.

Acts depicts Christians in an aggressive, determined pursuit of their Lord's goals: "Day after day, in the temple courts and from house to house, they never stopped teaching and proclaiming the good news that Jesus is the Christ."[13] It is impossible to read this book, and the rest of the New Testament, and evade the fact that all Christians are responsible for the success

of the movement—not only the special leaders. Luke's record of
the developing church is punctuated with comments on the
success of the movement.[14] The record also emphasizes the
need for reaching and strengthening disciples and churches, as
well as reaching new people.[15]

Productivity and Accountability

Jesus' emphasis on productivity among His followers is also
inescapable. He repeatedly compared His people to laborers,
stewards, and servants—all of whom are charged with accomplishing the work their master assigns. He also compared
them with branches that must bear fruit and salt that must
function or be useless.[16]

In many of His parables Jesus illustrated and advocated a
quality that one commentator has called "savvy." Our Lord
affirmed the shrewd ingenuity, if not the ethics, of the "unjust
steward."[17] In the "parable of the pounds"[18] the master entrusted a sum of money to each of his servants with the order to
"trade with it" until he returned. A literal rendering of the
order might properly read, "Be pragmatic" with the master's
affairs. The "parable of the talents"[19] introduces the variation
that not all the servants had the same potential and, therefore,
had varying degrees of responsibility. An acceptable result is
not measured against an absolute quantity. Even a small product can earn praise from the master, if the servant has done
what he could given his degree of opportunity. In any case, the
"bottom line" question is: Given your resources and opportunities, how much did you accomplish in serving God's purpose in your life, in the body of Christ, and in the world?

One servant failed to earn a profit. He attempted to justify
that fact by saying that he simply kept what had been entrusted
to him and was prepared to return it just as he had received it.
But the unprofitable servant was condemned. Mere survival is
an unacceptable alternative to success. Maintenance will not
take the place of productivity. Excuses will not substitute for
results. Faithfulness is equated with accomplishing the appointed task; worthlessness, with failure to try.

Key to the Success of the Church

Although Christianity and Marxism are poles apart in goals
and values, Karl Marx studied Christianity and its progress.

The Communist movement has demonstrated an almost un-
canny ability to identify principles of strength inherent in the
church and to use them effectively to achieve its purposes.
Christianity today might do well to reverse the process, identifying principles that have been perversely applied by Communism, and reclaiming them for victory in Christ's cause.

One such principle is that the individuals who comprise a
movement must be responsible for its success. This powerful
concept was once implemented in Christianity and then largely
laid aside. It is a concept that has been employed with great
effectiveness by other movements, including religious sects
and Communism.

This principle was clearly identified by a missionary in Latin
America, R. K. Strachan. Strachan studied the success of three
different movements that were all enjoying rapid growth:
Communism, the Jehovah's Witness movement, and the Pen-
tecostal movement. He then compared these movements with
the Christian church:

> The thing that intrigued me about these movements was that they
> were growing rapidly, whereas the traditional Christian Church,
> with all its formality, with all its proper life and all its orthodox
> doctrine, with all its organization, was more or less maintaining a
> level of stagnation, or else losing ground.
>
> After reading what books I could, making some visits, consulting,
> observing, asking, I arrived at a conclusion which to me was a sur-
> prise. I discovered that the doctrine in itself had nothing to do with
> the expansion of a movement; that neither did the form of worship;
> nor did the form of government; nor did the ministerial preparation,
> . . . nor the money that the organization might have available to
> spend in propaganda, nor was it its own particular emphasis—one
> thing alone could account for the growth of any movement.
>
> I tried then to reduce it to a proposition, and I arrived at this
> conclusion: that the expansion of any movement is in direct propor-
> tion to the success achieved in mobilizing and deploying its total
> membership in the continuous propagation of its beliefs.
>
> When I had arrived at that conclusion, so radical for me and
> revolutionary for my own ministry, I turned to the pages of the New
> Testament, and saw with open eyes what had been the strategy of
> the Holy Spirit working through the human instruments of His
> church to fulfill the eternal purpose of God—namely, that every
> person in every part of the world should have the opportunity to
> know the Gospel of the Lord Jesus Christ, and, believing, to be
> saved.[20]

A common maxim states the same idea: "All vital movements make converters out of their converts."

Douglas Hyde was a leading figure in the Communist cause until he arrived at the conclusion that the values and goals of Communism were intolerable evils. Turning his back on that movement, he looked to the church as the antithesis, expecting to find there as complete a commitment to Jesus Christ as he had known the Communists to have for their cause. The absence of this quality was startling; and so he began speaking to church people, appealing for the kind of intense sense of purpose he believed to be imperative. The essence of his ideas are contained in a small volume, *Dedication and Leadership*, which ought to be basic reading for Christians. In it, he says, "In my experience, the strength of Communism lies in its people and the way they are used. It is at this level that Communists have most to teach us."[21]

The following letter was written by a former eastern university student who went to Mexico and there became a Communist. It vividly articulates the commitment of the adherents of that movement:

> We communists have a high casualty rate. We are the ones who get shot, hung, lynched, tarred and feathered, jailed, slandered, fired from our jobs, and in every other way made as uncomfortable as possible. A certain percentage of us get killed or imprisoned. We live in virtual poverty. We turn back to the party every penny we make above what's absolutely necessary to keep alive.
>
> We don't have the time or money for many movies or concerts or T-bone steaks or decent homes or new cars. We've been described as fanatics. We are fanatics. Our lives are dominated by one great overshadowing factor, the struggle for world communism. We communists have a philosophy of life which no amount of money can buy.
>
> We have a cause to fight for, a definite purpose in life. We subordinate our petty personal selves into a great movement of humanity. If our personal lives seem hard or our egos appear to suffer through subordination to the party, then we are adequately compensated by the thought that each of us in his small way is contributing to something new and true and better for mankind.
>
> There is one thing for which I am in dead earnest and that is the communist cause. It is my life, my business, my religion, my hobby, my sweetheart, my wife and mistress, my bread and my meat. I work at it in the daytime and dream of it at night. Its hold on me grows, not lessens, as time goes on. Therefore I cannot carry on a friend-

ship, a love affair, or even a conversation without relating it to this force which both drives and guides my life. I evaluate people, books, ideas, and actions according to how they affect the communist cause and by their attitude toward it. I'm already in jail because of my ideas, and if necessary, I'm ready to go before a firing squad.[22]

There are enough members in the churches today to turn the tide of history for God, if every member would rise to the level of determination demonstrated by the Christians of the New Testament. Sailors have a saying: "When do we sail out of the doldrums? The day every man pulls hard on his oar." When will the church rise up as the mighty kingdom of God? The day every Christian and every congregation returns to the vitality of the people who first turned the world upside down for Christ.

The philosopher Kant said we should live in such a way that if everyone acted as we did, it would be well with the world. This principle certainly applies to the church. We should serve Christ and live for Him in such a way that, if everyone acted as we did, the kingdom would come and God's will would be done on earth, as it is in Heaven.

For Further Reading

Benjamin, Paul. The Growing Congregation. Cincinnati: Standard Publishing, 1975.

Christians, Clifford et. al. Who In The World? Grand Rapids: Eerdmans, 1972.

Edge, Findley. A Quest for Vitality in Religion. Nashville: Broadman Press, 1963.

Feucht, Oscar. Everyone a Minister. St. Louis: Concordia, 1974.

Gibbs, Mark and Ralph Morton. God's Frozen People. Philadelphia: Westminster Press, 1964.

_____. God's Lively People. Philadelphia: Westminster Press, 1971.

Halverson, Richard. How I Changed My Thinking About the Church. Grand Rapids: Zondervan, 1972.

Hyde, Douglas. Dedication and Leadership. Notre Dame, IN: University of Notre Dame, 1966.

Richards, Larry. A New Face for the Church. Grand Rapids: Zondervan, 1970.

Trueblood, Elton. The Company of the Committed. New York: Harper and Row, 1961.

Wagner, C. Peter. *Your Spiritual Gifts Can Help Your Church Grow.* Glendale: Regal, 1979.

Wentz, Frederick K. *Getting Into the Act.* Nashville: Abingdon, 1978.

---

[1]Numbers 13:33

[2]Findley B. Edge, *A Quest for Vitality in Religion* (Nashville: Broadman Press, 1963), p. 168. Used by permission.

[3]Matthew 22:2-14

[4]Elton Trueblood, *The Company of the Committed* (New York: Harper and Row, 1961), p. 59.

[5]Hans-Reudi Weber, *Salty Christians* (New York: Seabury Press, 1963), p. 25.

[6]*Ibid.*, p. 26.

[7]Matthew 13:44-46

[8]Matthew 16:24

[9]Luke 14:26-33

[10]Matthew 16:16

[11]Philippians 3:7-9

[12]Acts 4:23-30

[13]Acts 5:42

[14]Acts 2:47; 5:14; 6:7; 9:31; 11:21; 12:24; 13:49; 14:21; 19:10; 19:20; and others

[15]Acts 15:41; 16:5; 18:23

[16]John 15:1-8; Matthew 5:13

[17]Luke 16:1-10

[18]Luke 19:11-27

[19]Matthew 25:14-30

[20]W. Dayton Roberts, *Strachan of Costa Rica.* (Grand Rapids: Eerdmans, 1971), pp. 85, 86. Used by permission.

[21]Douglas Hyde, *Dedication and Leadership* (South Bend, IN: University of Notre Dame Press, 1966), p. 13.

[22]The original source of this quotation is unknown. This version appeared in *The Sunset Story* from the Sunset Church of Christ, Lubbock, Texas.

4

Equipping the People

As you read, think about these questions:
—How does the concept of "equipping" differ from conventional
  models of the church?
—How would a paid minister function in such a system?
—How would you diagram the structure of a congregation that has
  been organized to equip one another? How would you diagram the
  structure of your congregation?
—How would you design a program, such as Christian education, for
  your congregation so that it would equip them for service?

If the church is to fulfill its nature and achieve its purpose,
individual Christians must be committed to the tasks of:
  growing in personal Christlikeness,
  contributing to the building up of the body of Christ,
  and functioning as God's servants in the world.
In order to do these things well, Christians must be prepared.
No army would dare engage a highly significant task with raw,
untrained recruits.

The Equipping Model

Equipping may be a more accurate term than *nurture* or *con-*

servation to describe the second component of the Great Commission.

Nurture is defined as training or upbringing, but the idea that word often connotes is one of "care and feeding" or nourishment, without the aspect of rigorous discipline and training for a specific task. Nurture may become perennial nursemaiding rather than the leading of an individual toward mature functioning.

Conservation, another term sometimes applied to the second component of the Great Commission, can be even more static than nurture in its implications. Valuables are conserved in a bank vault; animals, in a game reserve; virgin land, in a park; books, in a library; works of art, in a museum. So the church may be thought of as simply the holding room where Christians are kept intact for Heaven.

Equipping is a dynamic, purpose-oriented concept. It means, "furnishing or preparing someone for service or action." This term also squares with such Scriptural concepts as Paul's figure of the Christian becoming fully armed and outfitted for spiritual warfare.[1] The Great Commission then becomes:

1. Recruiting people from the world to become part of Christ's community and movement, and

2. Equipping and mobilizing those people to live and function.

An Equipping Ministry

The equipping concept adjusts the focus of ministry. A minister who seeks to equip his people for service is not merely a chaplain who renders service to his clients. He works to enable other Christians to achieve God's purposes.

John Mills has described the conventional image of the local church ministry—an image that is more a product of the Western Protestant tradition than of Scriptural intent:

If we asked any group of children in our congregations to role play church for us, the leader would be the preacher and the rest would be told to listen. Communication is in only one direction— from pulpit to pews. Nothing is more important to us. The worship services are called "preaching services." Of course the one who preaches is then the main actor. The implication is that no one else can do anything worthwhile. The preacher is the main doer! . . .

This picture of the church has a built in system for lethargy. The preacher is the doer. If the church grows, it is to his glory. If it does not grow, then of course we need a new preacher.[2]

Mills is not seeking to diminish the role of preaching. Quite the contrary, he is questioning a static stereotype of preaching, in which the listeners are mere spectators or patrons of the preaching art. The alternative is preaching that deliberately strengthens people in the faith, helps them grow toward Biblical ideals, and prepares them to participate in the Christian movement.

Equipping is a mutual function rendered by all those in the body of Christ. It is also the special function of some. In the last few years, the fourth chapter of Ephesians has become prominent as a means for clarifying the roles of church members and leaders. Under the conventional mindset, verses 11-13 have been read as if leaders are to accomplish three objectives:

perfecting the saints,

doing the work of the ministry,

edifying the body of Christ.

Thus, the church becomes the recipient of a threefold leadership service. Even the punctuation in some versions seems to support the idea that the three items stand as parallel objectives. More adequate translations restore the original impact of the passage. The purpose of the leaders is:

to prepare God's people

for works of service,

so that the body of Christ may be built up.

The word in verse twelve often translated porfecting, preparing, or equipping contains the idea of preparing someone for a job or rendering someone functional. In God's design for the church, leaders are essential, but their task is not to do the work of the kingdom on behalf of other Christians; it is to equip other Christians to do the work of the kingdom.

Elton Trueblood was among the first to raise the current emphasis on the idea of an equipping ministry. He describes the congregation as a team in which every member is responsible for helping attain the goal. The minister functions as a *player-coach*, whose job it is to train and lead the team to victory—not a sideline coach, but a playing coach right alongside all the other team members.

Perhaps, suggests Trueblood, Christians should begin to think of the church building as the drill hall or armory where Christ's servants gather for encouragement, fellowship, and training. They develop strategies, they receive instructions, and they worship. Then they scatter to live out the gospel, to be the salt of the earth and the light of the world.

Such a change in style of ministry does require a shift in expectations a congregation holds for the minister. Some ministers have encountered problems in attempting to adopt this clarified image of their roles. In some cases they tried to redefine their function without first informing the congregation or generating a purposeful attitude among them. They confused their people by adopting new terminology without providing a solid rationale for it. Dissonance and confusion resulted.

In other cases, ministers failed to grasp the significance of the term *player*-coach. They attempted to become sideline coaches, locker room strategists, or armchair theoreticians. They sought to train and direct people from the study, the pulpit, and the classroom rather than at their side on the field of action. As a Christian among Christians, the minister shares the front-line ministry; in his special role, he assists them all to become more fully equipped.

The equipping concept should be taken one step further. The Christian who receives instruction or training should transmit to others what he has received. Paul was instructed of the Lord; he in turn instructed Timothy; and he directed Timothy to entrust this to "reliable men who will also be qualified to teach others."[3] Such a procedure produces an ever-expanding chain reaction.

Paul Benjamin, Director of the National Church Growth Research Center, in his book, *The Equipping Ministry*, gives a Biblical perspective for this concept of ministry. A study of this small, well-articulated volume would help a congregation work through these ideas. His earlier book, *The Growing Congregation*, has been used by many congregations to gain a more adequate point of view regarding the church and its role in the world.

Benjamin describes an image that dawned on his mind as he concluded an eighteen-year ministry. Driving out of town he suddenly realized that the preacher was leaving, the teacher was leaving, the pastor was leaving, the administrator was leaving, the evangelist was leaving, and the caller was leaving.

Most of the functions of the congregation were leaving in the person of one man. Benjamin vowed that if he were ever to be the minister of another congregation he would never carry out a function of ministry without training others to do it also. For example, in every hospital call or evangelistic call, he would try to arrange to take another Christian along to train that person to make such calls. The progress of Christ's cause would increase many-fold under such a model.

An Equipping Structure

John Mills also has pointed out how church organizational structures contribute to static conditions:

> At a recent rally of area churches, I placed newsprint on the wall and asked the churches to diagram their church organizational structures. A pyramid could have been placed over each diagram. This structure inherently breeds lethargy at the large base of the pyramid. These organizational systems say silently—"There is no working of the Holy Spirit among the saints. They are to do as they are told and pay the bills for what we plan."[4]

Even a theoretically correct church polity that does not equip the church to pursue its mission falls short of Biblical intention.

In visiting a congregation one Sunday, I arrived in the middle of one of the several morning worship services. As I parked in the large, well-filled lot, another car pulled into the next stall. The driver, recognizing me as a newcomer, introduced himself. He was an elder in the congregation, but seldom attended on Sunday morning because of a volunteer ministry he conducted on a nearby air base. He commented that he had formerly been a deacon in another congregation but was told that he must give up his ministry on the air base in order to be in his place at the church on Sunday morning, even though he had no particular function there. The structure of that congregation demanded conformity to officers, authority, and positions—in preference to productive ministry. In the present congregation his ministry was not only permitted but enthusiastically supported. This congregation's structure was equipping and dynamic.

One flourishing congregation has exchanged the pyramidal structure for a more Biblical and purposeful one. In its present diagram, the Christians who constitute the body of Christ are at the top, where the life and work of the church truly occur. These Christians are supported by units that would be called committees in many congregations. In this instance the units are called ministries, such as the ministry of worship, the ministry of benevolence, the ministry of Christian education, the ministry of evangelism, and so on.

Each of these ministries is directed by one or more deacons working with as many other people as needed. Each of these ministries seeks to enable the congregation to carry out the functions, not carry them out for the congregation. This level is supported by the elders and salaried staff members who give overall guidance and direction. Thus, the ministering congregation is equipped for various areas of ministry by functional units, which, in turn, are supported and equipped by the general overseers. The essential Biblical polity remains, and is highly functional.

Students of church growth have consistently identified addition of staff members as essential to keep growth from leveling off or declining. In notable exceptions, however, additional staff has not provided for growth. In these cases the church has very likely employed persons to do its work rather than to equip the church to do the work. Staff members must be seen as equippers of the saints, not as their delegates in ministry. Growing churches also multiply staff by bringing together people whose strengths are different; who supplement, rather than duplicate, one another.

An Equipping Program

Paul Benjamin points out the surprising opportunity the average congregation has to equip its people. The forty-year-old Christian who has been consistently active in the normal program of a congregation since age eighteen has been exposed to more than 4,000 hours of preaching and teaching. That same eighteen-year-old could have received a bachelor's degree in 1,800 hours of college classroom instruction, a Master of Divinity in an additional 1,350 hours, and a doctorate in a total of 4,000 hours. It is obvious that churches do not make the most of their opportunities to equip God's people for competent service. All too often the programs of churches are not designed and carried out with the deliberate strategy they deserve.

If the competencies that make Christians effective servants of Christ were identified; if the necessary knowledge, attitudes, and skills were defined; and if programs were carefully designed to meet well-articulated objectives—the productivity of Christ's servants could be multiplied. The congregation referred to in the previous section has developed such a program. Worship services, Sunday-school classes, various study events, and the numerous meetings and functions of the church move toward clear-cut goals, preparing the members in specific ways to live as Christians and serve Christ effectively.

James Kennedy describes his early years in the ministry as far from this ideal. Week after week he impressed on his congregation that they should be leading others to become Christians, but he never prepared them to do it. As a result, his congregation dwindled from more than 40 to 18 persons. When he did begin preparing others to evangelize, he discovered that he himself first had to learn how to evangelize. He then trained others who, in turn, trained others. The result has been described as an evangelistic explosion.[5]

This is an example of a process often called *discipling*. It has been demonstrated to be highly effective in developing growing, functioning, capable Christians.[6] Kennedy uses on-the-job training, supplemented with classroom and private study, to equip his people. Activities such as Sunday school are clearly focused on the objectives of that congregation. This kind of specific, action oriented training stands in stark contrast to the always-preparing-but-never-doing programs so often found in congregations.

Eleanor Daniel, practitioner and teacher of Christian education, described her discovery of a reason people suddenly lose interest and drop out after years of Sunday school attendance. It happened on a flight from the United States to India. During the flight of some 24 hours over the Atlantic, Europe and the Near East, meals were served according to local time. By the passengers' "internal clocks," the meals came at odd times— such as dinner at 4:00 a.m. The schedule also compressed two days' meals into one 24-hour period. All the while, the passengers were inactive. By the last meal or two, people could not bear the thought of eating again. Intake without activity became too much to endure. In reflecting on this experience, Professor Daniel thought of the church people who come week after week to the Sunday school and are fed on the Word but are not led into active use of what they have received. No wonder, then, that people eventually have had enough and want no more.

Curriculum

In education, the curriculum is the means by which students are helped to move toward the objectives of knowledge, attitude, skills, and conduct. It is a combination of information and experiences that will assist the learner to move from where he is toward the objectives. The church ought to ask such curricular questions as:

What would a mature, fully effective Christian know, understand, believe, value, and be able to do?

How would he live and act toward the church, other Christians, and the rest of the world?

Where are our people now, in comparison?

What experiences and information will help us move from where we are toward the ideal?

What can be done to achieve these objectives through morning and evening worship services,
> Sunday school,
> midweek studies, and
> other existing units and activities?

What new programs must be developed, and what resources can be used?

A curriculum must be locally designed to meet specific needs. Some large congregations develop their own materials, but this is impractical, if not impossible, for all but a few. The other congregations select from the plethora of published materials available today. The error many (perhaps most) churches make is that they fail to realize that published materials are the raw materials for the curriculum. Lumber, bricks, windows, doors, and shingles from the lumber yard are not a house. They are delivered to the site as components; the builder must put them together to create a house. Christian materials from a publisher are not a curriculum; they must be selected and constructed "on the site" to meet the needs and objectives of a specific congregation in order to equip its people for effective living and serving.

One particularly effective congregation has an elaborate structure of Christian education. It has identified seven areas of ministry in which its people may be involved. Every member is counseled and helped to select the particular ministry in which he or she will concentrate. They are then enrolled in a series of educational experiences to equip them. They are also placed alongside experienced people as apprentices in that area of ministry where they move toward mature competency. The curriculum consists of a general Biblical core as well as specialized studies and training experiences in the various areas of ministry.

When the program of the church is rigorously viewed as equipping the saints for service, then the gathering-scattering rhythm will function properly.[7] The church will gather to prepare for specific purposes, then it will scatter to implement those purposes. Like an army it will assemble for briefing and training, then it will scatter to win the victory on the front line. Frederick Wentz says that the church needs to view itself as paratroopers dropped behind enemy lines on Monday with the expectation of making their way back to the supply depot on the following Sunday.[8]

Conclusion

A. Leonard Griffith says that the reorientation of the church to equipping its people is the great necessity of our age:

> No, it has not yet caught on, this idea whose time has come in our generation, but when it does catch on, there will be a renewal of life in the churches comparable in its impact to the Protestant Reformation and the Evangelical Revival. It will revolutionize the concept of a local congregation which in many places still resembles a theatre and audience made up of critical spectators who believe that they have performed something meritorious by their mere presence at worship. Instead of being the sum total of Christian responsibility, Sunday worship will be seen as but the beginning of Christian responsibility. A community of Christians will come together on the Lord's Day, and one of their number, because he has been trained and set apart to interpret the Word of God, will brief his fellow-workers and help them to begin a new week in their ministry. They will share in the world's labour, sitting at desks, counting money, operating machines or disciplining little children, but always the real priority will be given to the fact that they are volunteers in a Christian army who have accepted the Lordship of Jesus Christ. They will say, as William Carey said, "I cobble shoes to earn my bread and butter, but my business is to serve God."[9]

For Further Reading

Benjamin, Paul. *The Equipping Ministry.* Cincinnati: Standard, 1978.
Brown, Neil. *Laity Mobilized: Reflections on Church Growth in Japan and Other Lands.* Grand Rapids: Eerdmans, 1971.
Edge, Findley. *The Greening of the Church.* Waco, TX: Word, 1971.
Johnson, Douglas W. *The Care and Feeding of Volunteers.* Nashville: Abingdon, 1978.
Savage, John. *The Apathetic and Bored Church Member.* (LEAD) Consultants, Inc. P.O. Box 311, Pittsford, New York 14534, 1976.
Trueblood, Elton. *The Company of the Committed.* New York: Harper and Row, 1961.
_____. *Your Other Vocation.* New York: Harper and Brothers, 1952.

---

[1]Ephesians 6:10-18
[2]John Mills, "Equipping and Doing" (An address delivered at the North American Christian Convention, St. Louis, MO: July, 1979).
[3]2 Timothy 2:2
[4]Mills, *op. cit.*
[5]D. James Kennedy, *Evangelism Explosion* (Wheaton, IL: Tyndale, 1970.)
[6]Especially notable sources for this concept are: *The Master Plan of Evangelism,* by Robert Coleman (Old Tappan, NJ: Revell, 1963); and *The Training of the Twelve,* by A. B. Bruce (New York: Harper and Brothers).
[7]Paul Benjamin, *The Growing Congregation.* Lincoln, IL: Lincoln Christian College Press, 1972.
[8]Frederick Wentz, *Getting Into the Act* (Nashville: Abingdon, 1978), p. 34.
[9]Griffith, A. Leonard. *What is a Christian?* (New York: Abingdon Press, 1962), p. 170. Used by permission.

5

Fellowship

As you read, think about these questions:
—In what way is Christian fellowship a unique relationship?
—If Christian fellowship were fully operating, what would relation-
ships among Christians be like?
—How is Christian fellowship part of the goal that churches are to
achieve?
—What hinders the full operation of Christian fellowship in churches?
Which of these hindrances do you observe in your congregation?

If you have any encouragement from being united with Christ, if
any comfort from his love, if any fellowship with the Spirit, if any
tenderness and compassion, then make my joy complete by being
like-minded, having the same love, being one in spirit and purpose.[1]

Few living creatures can survive, let alone flourish, without
interaction with others of their kind. Human beings are especially interdependent, requiring more elaborate relationships
than nearly any other form of life. It is not surprising, then, that
Christians have a deep and imperative spiritual need for one
another. The Biblical term for the ideal relationship among
Christians is *fellowship*. It is a unique relationship, profoundly
interconnected with the purpose of the church.

The Uniqueness of Christian Fellowship

Animals have herd instincts, but cannot develop the quality of relationships human beings experience. Likewise, the non-Christian cannot experience the quality of relationship Christians can share. Christian fellowship is unique in the world—not just natural human association made better, but community of a different kind. It constitutes a working model of the relationship God intended for people and a microcosm of Heaven itself.

If grains of sand are poured together, they touch, yet remain apart. This is descriptive of human community. If drops of water are poured together, they flow together, each drop partaking of the characteristics of every other drop until they are one. This is descriptive of Christian fellowship,[2] except that the oneness shared by Christians does not imply a loss of individuality.

Jesus initiated fellowship by choosing twelve men *to be with Him.*[3] He gave a great deal of attention to developing among these men the particular kind of interaction in which they could mature toward God's ideals. In addition to learning precepts from Jesus, this band of disciples discovered by *experience* how to relate to Him and to each other. They received from Him the revolutionary new commandment, "Love one another. As I have loved you, so you must love one another." This, He said, would be the identifying mark by which His people could be recognized.[4]

The uniqueness of the relationship in the Christian community is sometimes dulled in the common usage of the term *fellowship.* The word is often applied to functions or relationships that do not begin to measure up to the Biblical ideal. In an attempt to recapture a sense of that unique quality, some people revert to the word used in the original Biblical language, *koinonia.*

The relationship learned by the inner circle of disciples carried over naturally into the church and was described by that expressive word *koinonia.* This quality became the hallmark of the early church. The astonished world had never before seen such a relationship among people. Here was a group of people who sincerely cared for each other as much as they cared for themselves, who were sensitive to each other's feelings and needs, who were together and "of one heart and mind."[5] In this remarkable relationship, Christians shared each other's hurts, weaknesses, personal problems, material needs, aspirations, prayer concerns, and victories. They associated in a climate of acceptance, openness, encouragement, assistance, support, and trust. They became more truly brothers and sisters than if they had been born of the same human parents.[6] It was as though their lives were welded together.

Christian fellowship becomes even more distinctive as the sense of community among human beings in the world erodes. Society has become so mobile, so "things" centered, so preoccupied with self-interest that the sense of belonging to one another or of commitment to one another is slipping away. The quality of rugged individualism that was once idealized is deteriorating into a preoccupation with self, a militant self-centeredness, a "me-ism" that can turn people, so to speak, into snarling animals. Crime rates soar as the every-man-for-himself philosophy intensifies. Individuals come to the brink of despair, but no one seems to care. A person dies before the eyes of onlookers who do not lift a hand to help, lest they become "involved." Individuals grow more lonely, fearful, hopeless, and desperate as the human community disintegrates into isolation. Communications break down as people do not (and seem determined they *will* not) understand each other's point of view. These trends alarm leaders who search desperately for ways to restore the sense of responsible community to society. Meanwhile, desperate people turn for sympathy and help to bartenders, hairdressers, psychiatrists, occultists, club members, or anyone else they can find. The results are often more negative than the original problem.

Fellowship and Purpose

Christian fellowship is profoundly interconnected with the purpose of the church. In the first place, restoring a particular kind of relationship among Christians in the body of Christ is itself an element of the divine purpose. Secondly, the quality of fellowship among its members intensifies or diminishes the degree to which a church succeeds in helping Christians grow and fulfilling its mission to the world. Finally, purposefulness has a reciprocal effect on the quality of fellowship among Christians.

Fellowship as a Divine Objective

The quality of human association intended by God, but lost by man's sin, is restored in Christian fellowship.

Jesus devoted much attention to the subject of relationships among His followers. This, He said, is the second most important subject in the world, outranked only by one's relationship with God. As a matter of fact, one's relationship with other people deeply affects his relationship to God:

> If we claim to have fellowship with him yet walk in the darkness, we lie and do not live by the truth. But if we walk in the light, as he is in the light, we have fellowship with one another, and the blood of Jesus, His Son, purifies us from all sin. . . . Anyone who claims to be in the light but hates his brother is still in the darkness. Whoever loves his brother lives in the light, and there is nothing in him to make him stumble. But whoever hates his brother is in the darkness and walks around in the darkness; he does not know where he is going, because the darkness has blinded him.[7]

In the body of Christ the abilities of each member complement the abilities of other members, so that the body is fully equipped and functions harmoniously. "God has combined the members of the body . . . so that there should be no division in the body, but that its parts should have equal concern for each other. If one part suffers, every part suffers with it; if one part is honored, every part rejoices with it."[8] Paul says further that Christians are to be humble, gentle, patient, and helpful to one another. They are to consider their own abilities as gifts of God, to be used in ministering to each other. Since each Christian has needs and others have particular abilities to meet those needs, ministry is shared in the struggle to become all that God wants for His people. Thus the whole church, and each member of it, will grow to strength and maturity, resembling Jesus himself.[9]

The apostle Peter urges Christians to treat one another in the following way:

> Above all, love each other deeply, because love covers a multitude of sins. Offer hospitality to one another without grumbling. Each one should use whatever gift he has received to serve others, faithfully administering God's grace in its various forms. If anyone speaks, he should do it as one speaking the very words of God. If anyone serves, he should do it with the strength God provides, so

that in all things God may be praised through Jesus Christ. To him be the glory and power for ever and ever. Amen.[10]

Christians live not for themselves alone, but for one another and for the whole body in a caring relationship. Christians in the New Testament era would die for each other; how, then, could they think of calling their possessions their own if one of their number was genuinely in need?

"One another" is a recurring phrase in New Testament letters to Christians. It is used to exhort the followers of Jesus to:

love one another (1 John 3:11)
instruct one another (Romans 15:14)
encourage one another (1 Thessalonians 5:11)
provoke one another to love and good works (Hebrews 10:24)
rejoice with one another (Romans 12:15; 1 Corinthians 12:26)
weep with one another (Romans 12:15)
forgive one another (Ephesians 4:32)
forbear one another (Ephesians 4:2)
confess their faults to one another (James 5:16)
pray for one another. (James 5:16)

These ministries are exchanged by Christians as a part of their fellowship in the Spirit.

Fellowship is love applied.[11] Because God loves us, we are enabled to love Him and other people. Thus, the quality of God's relationship to man in Christ also becomes the quality of Christians' relationships with one another.

Fellowship is more than simple human interaction. It has a plus factor: the presence of Christ.[12] When Christians interact in Christ's name, He is in each of them, drawing them together, and He is among them.

Fellowship and Personal Growth

In order to grow properly, Christian lives must be rooted and focused in the Christian community. Fellowship provides the climate for personal maturation toward Christlikeness.

Groups of people exert a powerful influence upon the individuals who constitute them. Groups establish norms for corporate and individual thought and behavior; and, through the socializing process, mold the lives of their members to conform to these norms.

Norms consist of two kinds, stated (the group's formal

ideals) and operating (its actual attitudes and expectations).
The two are not always identical, and where discrepancies
exist between them, the operating norms are the "real" ones
that prevail and are passed on to newcomers.

Most churches, for example, will talk about the high challenges of Jesus' teachings, but in many congregations performance norms fall far short of these ideals. The fervent new
Christian who enters a congregation where performance norms
are low begins to think that his intensity is naive, and that the
performance he observes is the way Christianity is really supposed to be. On the other hand, a congregation in which actual
practice approaches the Biblical ideal wields a positive transforming influence in the lives of its people.

Values, attitudes, and standards of conduct are transmitted
more through relationships than through precept. Thus, ideals
are said to be more "caught" than "taught." This happens
through fellowship.

Peripheral church members who keep their relationships
rooted outside the church show little growth and maintain a
tenuous contact with Christian ideals. The individual who is
not enfolded in a strong sense of community is hindered in his
ability to grow up in Christ, to implement seriously the details
of the Christian way in his life, or to function effectively as
God's agent in the world.

When functioning properly, fellowship provides the conditions under which Christians receive the help they need to
incorporate Biblical principles into their day-to-day lives. Individuals learn to face and deal with their problems and weaknesses, begin using their gifts for Christ, seek understanding,
receive encouragement, and attempt new ways of thinking and
behaving. They are enabled to remove the "beams from their
own eyes" instead of defensively looking for "specks in the
eyes of others." They can face what they are and who they are,
and they can open their lives to the transforming grace of God.
The faith they learn with their minds becomes real in their
actions. The Bible becomes more than mere information; it becomes the living, powerful Word, the exciting guidance of God
to be followed and shared with other people. Prayer takes on
new power as brothers and sisters in Christ pray for and with
each other about mutual concerns. Christians become the
ministers of God to one another; as fellow aliens in this world,
they help one another not only to survive but to succeed. The

climate of this fellowship is described in the letter to Christians in Ephesus:

> I urge you to live a life worthy of the calling you have received. Be completely humble and gentle; be patient, bearing with one another in love. . . .
> Therefore, each of you must put off falsehood, and speak truth-fully to his neighbor, for we are all members of one body. In your anger do not sin: Do not let the sun go down while you are still angry, and do not give the devil a foothold. He who has been steal-ing must steal no longer, but must work, doing something useful with his own hands, that he may have something to share with those in need. Do not let any unwholesome talk come out of your mouths, but only what is helpful for building others up according to their needs, that it may benefit those who listen. And do not grieve the Holy Spirit of God, with whom you were sealed for the day of re-demption. Get rid of all bitterness, rage and anger, brawling and slander, along with every form of malice. Be kind and compassion-ate to one another, forgiving each other, just as in Christ God forgave you.[13]

Fellowship and Mission

In addition to its other functions, fellowship also forms the base of operations from which Christians undertake the task of being God's agents to the world around them. It serves as a "launching pad" from which the church scatters to take its influence to every corner of society. In fellowship, the indi-vidual Christian's responsibilities become clear and compel-ling. His commitment, courage, and motivation gain strength. Members of the body of Christ provide each other with the support necessary to venture out to be Christ's witnesses, the salt of the earth, the light of the world.

Those who have tried to start a charcoal fire in a grill know that one cannot scatter the individual pieces of charcoal and get them to take fire. Eventually, the pieces will have to be scattered in order to function, but first they must be heaped together and ignited. When the fire has penetrated the mass and the pieces have been ignited by each other, they can be scattered to do their task. This illustrates the way Christians share fellowship in preparation for serving God through their individual lives. In view of this principle, Elton Trueblood has described the church as The Incendiary Fellowship.[14]

This outward orientation of fellowship keeps groups of

Christians from becoming "in" groups or cliques. Otherwise groups can engage in self-satisfying but fruitless, and perhaps unhealthy, processes. Fellowship that does not face outward to the tasks Jesus gave His people is less than New Testament *koinonia*. In the beginning days of the church, fellowship was a prime contributor to the vitality that exploded outward, sweeping the world in a wave of evangelism. Christian unity is sometimes thought of as an abstraction, or as a static state of affairs. In reality, it is an inherently dynamic concept that describes Christians as joined together in a common cause. The unity for which Jesus prayed will cause the world to believe.[15]

Every powerful movement is able to develop a solidarity among their constituents in pursuit of its purposes. A perverse application of this principle is observable among radical religious sects in which leaders employ solidarity to manipulate their followers to a degree that astonishes outsiders.

Fellowship Developed by Purposefulness

Not only does fellowship contribute to accomplishing the purpose of the church, it is also *created* by people's commitment to a common purpose. If individuals are dominated by different purposes, they have very little in common and do not develop strong relationships; but people who share a powerful commitment to the same purpose are united by a strong bond.

Misguided attempts to develop fellowship among Christians have produced, at best, a pseudo-fellowship. Sometimes the result has been a maudlin, humanistic, directionless sentimentalism. *Koinonia*, on the other hand, is more akin to the deep commitment soldiers develop for each other when they fight side by side on the battlefield. When Christian relationships lack clear commitment to a common purpose, they develop along counterfeit lines and may deteriorate.

The millers who once ran gristmills had to be careful to keep grain between the millstones at all times. Otherwise, the great stones would grind each other to pieces. The mill would destroy itself if not engaged in its intended function. A parallel may be seen in the relationships among Christians. If the church is not properly engaged in accomplishing its purpose, it may grind destructively upon itself. This is one reason churches become embroiled in internal friction and sometimes manifest relationships that are as corrosive as those that exist among people of the world.

Developing Fellowship in the Church

Christian fellowship is fragile. It requires patience to develop and care to maintain. Churches must consciously and consistently work to strengthen this quality among its people.

One of the earliest problems in the church was division. Dissent threatened to fragment the unity of Christians in Galatia and Corinth. The letters of Paul to these churches deal stringently with this problem. Jealousy, pride, prejudice, and self-centeredness were at the roots of such fractures.

Contemporary church relationships are often impersonal and sometimes negative. Many ecclesiastical forms foster a platform-audience arrangement; people attend services more as spectators than as participants; and an atmosphere develops that is tainted with aloofness.

With considerable insight, Larry Richards has applied to the church the sociological concepts of *gesellschaft* and *gemeinschaft* (association and community).[16] In the former, people are organizationally related; in the latter, they are intensely and personally related. Unless specific effort is exerted, church relationships can easily lose the quality of community and deteriorate into mere association.

Church activities are often so formally arranged that relationships go no deeper than human civility. Functions become a kind of religious art form for the exercise of musical talent, oratory, and ritual. People fulfill their responsibilities as Christians by the simple fact of attending. Members know each other only casually, maintaining "white-glove" distance which consists of polite greetings and small talk.

Current American culture also works against Christian fellowship. Under prevailing social norms, only weaklings admit they need other people, seek support, or let other people get close to them. Thomas Harris, author of *I'm OK—You're OK*, has suggested that human beings avoid close relationships out of defensiveness. Because we disapprove of ourselves and feel we are not what we ought to be, we cannot risk criticism or disapproval from others. We are afraid of exposing our real selves, so we keep our distance and devise ways to avoid getting close to each other. Rituals, Harris says, are a socially programmed use of time where everybody agrees to do the same thing in such a way that they are safe because there is no commitment, no involvement, and the outcome is known in advance. They are designed to get a group of people through the hour without having to get close to anyone. Such relationships are a long way from unconditional acceptance, love, and trust, but they sometimes prevail among Christians.

Consider how, for example, weddings and funerals have been formalized from a function of fellowship into ritual. It would be natural for Christian people entering into marriage to want their Christian friends to share with them in a time of joy and prayer. This is a function of fellowship. Little fellowship, however, is retained in cultural forms that have developed around weddings. In similar fashion the funeral has been so stylized that one can hardly recognize the banding together of Christians to affirm their faith and strengthen one another in sorrow.

Koinonia ought to unify Christians all over the world in one body and unite local groups of Christians into strong communities, but most Christians find they need a small circle of intimates with whom they can share person-to-person. Congregations are discovering ways of fostering a greater sense of community through small groups. Existing classes and other structures can help provide for fellowship in the church, but many Christians need a still more specific circle of eight to twelve Christians with whom they can develop more completely the dynamics of Christian relationships. These may be formally arranged groups or small informal circles of contact. Some people fear that these small units of fellowship might fragment the church. The opposite is more likely to be the case because, as the few intensify their fellowship, they become more and more concerned about the many.

Robert Yawberg has described the results of a revitalization in Christian fellowship:

> Many Christians across the land are discovering the simple New Testament concept of fellowship. They are praying together with other Christians in homes, offices, restaurants, and schools. As in the days of the early church, they are searching the Word of God for truth. There is a spontaneous sharing of insights in an atmosphere of freedom and acceptance. People are learning to love one another, just as they are; and they are helping each other to feel that they do not have to have perfect understanding before attempting to express their ideas.
>
> These groups are not intended to take the place of corporate worship, but as in New Testament days, they provide a time for growth

and involvement between Sundays. They become the spawning ground for renewal of faith. Those who have been Christians all their lives find a deepening of their faith. New followers of the way discover the joy of Bible reading and prayer that helps them to mature. From there, they are led to witness. As Christ becomes real in the fellowship of a small action group, He must be shared with others.[17]

For Further Reading

Drakeford, John. *Farewell to the Lonely Crowd*. Waco, TX: Word, 1969.
Getz, Gene. *The Measure of a Church*. Glendale: Regal, 1975.
_____. *Building Up One Another*. Raleigh, NC: Victor, 1977.
Halverson, Richard. *How I Changed My Thinking About the Church*. Grand Rapids: Zondervan, 1972.
Richards, Larry. *A New Face for the Church*. Grand Rapids: Zondervan, 1970.
_____. *Becoming One in the Spirit*. Raleigh, NC: Victor, 1973.
Schaeffer, Francis A. *The Church at the End of the 20th Century*. Downers Grove, IL: Inter-Varsity, 1970.
Stedman, Ray. *Body Life*. Glendale, CA: Regal, 1972.
Trueblood, Elton. *The Incendiary Fellowship*. New York: Harper and Row, 1967. Victor Books.
Wagner, C. Peter. *Your Church Can Grow*. Glendale: Regal, 1976.
Williams, Robert A. *A Place to Belong*. Grand Rapids: Zondervan, 1972.
Worley, Robert C. *A Gathering of Strangers: Understanding the Life of Your Church*. Philadelphia: Westminster, 1976.

---

[1]Philippians 2:1, 2
[2]John 17:20-23
[3]Mark 3:14
[4]John 13:34, 35
[5]Acts 4:32
[6]Mark 3:33-35
[7]1 John 1:6, 7; 2:9-11
[8]1 Corinthians 12:24-26
[9]Ephesians 4:1-7, 11-16
[10]1 Peter 4:8-11
[11]1 John 4:7, 8, 19-21
[12]Matthew 18:19, 20
[13]Ephesians 4:1, 2, 25-32
[14]Elton Trueblood, *The Incendiary Fellowship* (New York: Harper and Row, 1967).

[15]John 17:21

[16]Lawrence O. Richards, *A New Face for the Church* (Grand Rapids: Zondervan, 1970) p. 51.

[17]Robert Yawberg, *Growing Together in Christian Fellowship* (Cincinnati: Standard Publishing, 1972) pp. 2, 3.

6

Spiritual Power

As you read, think about these questions:
—What is the relationship between the nature of the church and its dependency on God for its power?
—What conditions are necessary for a church to experience God's empowering?
—Why are Christians and churches sometimes relatively powerless?
—How would you describe your congregation in terms of being empowered by God?

When the church began, the followers of Jesus were a small congregation of some 120 people. Many were common people, lacking social, political, or economic leverage. Two of their principal leaders were viewed as "unschooled, ordinary men." They lived in a small, rather insignificant outpost of the Roman Empire. Their Lord's commission to recruit the peoples of the world as His disciples might have seemed naive, if not ludicrous. Yet they undertook to do exactly that, in spite of overwhelming obstacles.

Three thousand new people joined them the day they began their mission. Their number increased daily, soon reaching 5,000. Efforts to stamp out the movement only resulted in further rapid growth. Soon a large number of the Jewish priests joined the movement, and ultimately its prime human adversary, Saul of Tarsus, became its most effective proponent. The gathering wave of evangelism broke over the cities and provinces of the Empire, including Rome itself. To this day, no influence in the world is greater than that of the church.

Divine Resources Required

Christianity is more than a human movement using only natural processes; it is supernatural in origin and power. Human ability and effort alone cannot account for its character and accomplishments. God fills human vessels, indwells them, and works through them. He is both the commissioner and enabler of the church, and of individual Christians.

God created the church in order to achieve His eternal purpose. He willed its existence from the beginning of the world.[1] He provided for its initiation through the death, resurrection, and high priestly ministry of His Son.[2] He brought it into being through the power of His Spirit.[3] He gave it the task of making people disciples of His Son through the complementary processes of evangelism and edification.

Jesus' promise in the Commission—"And surely I will be with you always, to the very end of the age"—is assured to those who are engaged in carrying out the task assigned.[4] The longer ending of Mark's Gospel exemplifies the fulfillment of that promise: "Then the disciples went out and preached everywhere, and the Lord worked with them and confirmed his word by the signs that accompanied it."[5]

At the time of His return to Heaven, Jesus instructed His people to wait for the empowering of the Holy Spirit before undertaking His Commission.[6] His work was not to be accomplished by human resources alone. R.E.O. White has suggested that the book of Acts might well be called "Acts of the Ascended Lord." Luke, the author of Acts, says that his first book (the Gospel) concerned all that Jesus *began* to do and teach. Acts, says White, "shows Him still empowering, superintending, stretching forth His hand to heal, closing or opening doors for the Gospels, 'standing by' His servants in prison, on board ship, and in Caesar's court."[7]

The church is built up through the efforts of men; but although one may "plant" and another may "water," success ultimately depends upon God.[8] Paul identifies Christ as the head of the church "from whom the whole body, supported and held together by its ligaments and sinews, grows as God causes it to grow."[9] And it is the Spirit that enables human beings to join together in becoming the body of Christ, bringing to that body their complementary abilities in such a way that all its functions are provided.[10]

In Christ's mission to the world, man labors, but it is God who has given the gospel, which is His power to salvation.[11] Paul tells the Thessalonian Christians, "Our gospel came to you not simply with words, but also with power, with the Holy Spirit and with deep conviction."[12] In a similar way he reminds the Corinthian Christians, "I came to you in weakness and fear, and with much trembling. My message and my preaching were not with wise and persuasive words, but with a demonstration of the Spirit's power, so that your faith might not rest on men's wisdom, but on God's power."[13]

Purpose and Power

The church is the instrument God created and commissioned as the means through which He presently pursues His purposes in the world. The church, then, can expect Him to provide the resources necessary for its task.

Certain miraculous dimensions of God's empowering of the church were temporary, intended only for the founding era of the church. But the necessity for God's indwelling and empowering of His people has not changed. God's *style* of empowering may have changed, but not the *fact* of it. Vital Christians and congregations know that God is at work today and that He is involved with *them* in accomplishing His will. They seek to do His will, and they seek to be infused with His power in doing so.

In Jesus' parable of the servants, the man who best exploited the stewardship entrusted to him was given more, while the unproductive servant lost even what he had. To the bystanders' objections, the master replied, "I tell you that to everyone who has, more will be given, but as for the one who has nothing, even what he has will be taken away."[14]

As in the case of Christian fellowship, the pursuit of purpose and divine power occupy a mutually reinforcing relationship. God provides the power to accomplish His purpose *as His people fulfill that purpose.* Without His power they cannot achieve

His purpose—without their fullest commitment, God does not supply His fullest power. The presence of God is less likely to be experienced by those who seek to climb the spiritual heights for private experience than by those who plunge into the tasks God has set before them. Those who are most engaged in bringing the gospel with all its power into the lives of others become more fully partakers of that power themselves.

Through the ages, the Holy Spirit has been inseparably linked with God's pursuit of His purposes. The Holy Spirit came upon the prophets of the Old Testament to commission and enable them to serve God's interests, not simply to bring them spiritual satisfaction. On the contrary, their lives were often upset and rearranged for God's use. We sometimes envy their power and their accomplishments. We can more properly expect such results when we match their commitment to God's interests.

Persons err when they seek the activity of the Spirit primarily for the sake of personal gratification. When people feel they must engage in spiritual gymnastics to influence the activity of the Spirit in their lives, they may be attempting to divert the Spirit to their own ends rather than joining Him for God's ends.

It is more likely that the Holy Spirit's activity will cause people's lives to be spent in Christ's labors. And it is even more likely that persons whose lives are already so invested will receive such enabling of the Spirit. When the power already present is used in the purpose for which it is most directly intended, greater power follows. Persons who line up with God's goals are naturally lined up with the direction of His energies. If they open themselves to Him, those energies will fill and flow through them.

The Current Scene

The potential for spiritual power and achievement remains a great unexplored frontier for many Christians and churches. Many congregations seldom venture beyond human parameters.

All too often congregations demonstrate a low level of accomplishment, operating routinely on the level of what is "possible," "practical," "realistic," "feasible," or "desirable." Whatever is accomplished is done on the basis of human wisdom, resources, ingenuity, and effort alone. They plan, make decisions, and operate as if all were up to them, as if no potential outside themselves really existed, as if God were remote to the present time and place. They operate on a kind of "practical humanism," repeating the words about the power of God but not acting on the truth thereof. An observer has suggested that if God ever went out of business, some churches would never know the difference.

In his book, *Authentic Christianity*, Ray Stedman compares the man who tries to live the Christian life solely by the strength of his own human resources to a man who buys a car and then tries to operate it without using the motor. When asked how he likes his new car, the owner replies, "Oh, it's a tremendous car. Look at the upholstery, and get an eyeful of this color, and, oh yes, listen to the horn—what a great horn this car has. But I do find it rather exhausting! It goes downhill beautifully, but if there is even the slightest rise in the pavement, I find myself panting and struggling and groaning. It is very difficult to push uphill."[15]

No matter how much instruction he receives on the subject, "How to Push a Car Successfully," the car will perform at only a fraction of its potential.

Such a comparison is valid on a corporate as well as an individual level. Congregations struggle to push forward and upward, all the while neglecting the spiritual power available to them. Most churches, of course, do not totally neglect the divine power source, but few totally utilize it. This occurs for several reasons.

First, members of a congregation may be ignorant of what God's purposes actually are. Some religious bodies have a low view of the nature and authority of Scripture. The Bible has been neglected in the pulpit, in the Sunday-school classroom, and, consequently, in the home, to the extent that many congregations really have no idea what God's will for them is. It is little wonder, then, that they lack spiritual power.

Second, members of a congregation may be intellectually aware of the teaching of Scripture but fail to act accordingly. People may know correct doctrine by mental assent without making the doctrine their own. Churches whose members lack an operational conviction concerning Scripture do not pursue God's purposes of evangelism and edification, even if they know what those purposes are.

Third, church members may be intellectually aware of the

teaching of Scripture but fail to act accordingly because they lack faith in themselves, or in God, or both. McGavran and Arn emphasize the relationship between a congregation's faith in its ability to reach out and grow, and its effectiveness in actively pursuing God's purposes. A much more serious hindrance, however, is that of a lack of faith in God:

> Radiant personal faith on the part of younger and older churches, ministers and missionaries, laymen and youth, is an irreplaceable factor. Everything else can be there, but if this is absent, church growth scarcely ever occurs. Conversely, when there is authentic spiritual fire all kinds of difficult circumstances are surmounted.[16]

Faith in God's willingness and ability to work through His people to accomplish His ends is vital because it motivates the Christian to be unafraid of failure and public embarrassment. He can move boldly and bravely forward, attempting big things for God and expecting great things from God.

Fourth, some congregations fail to pursue God's purposes because, although their members understand that God is working to save men and develop them as His disciples, they falsely believe that He has no active part for them in this task.

> Some people start from the presupposition that, as God is sovereign, "whatever will be will be;" and that as long as we exist merely as a Christian presence in the world, we can leave the rest to Him. This is surely to confuse the immediate and ultimate, and to overlook our responsibility as his servants. Of course, the ultimate end lies with God, but in the meantime, we may either help or hinder His immediate purpose.[17]

When this type of misunderstanding of the sovereignty of God prevails in a congregation, that congregation may reach the point where it merely sits back to watch how God decides to accomplish His will. It thus fails to pursue His purposes and consequently is deprived of the spiritual power it could have enjoyed had its members given their best efforts in an attempt to evangelize the lost and edify the saved.

While some congregations do not actively pursue God's purposes, others fail to experience the fullness of God's power because they pursue His purposes with an attitude of self-sufficiency rather than one of dependence on God. Contemporary American congregations are especially susceptible to this attitude, because of the way the American culture idealizes the independent, self-made individual. The Christian in America is subtly tempted to believe that he can be the kind of Christian he should be on the strength of his own human abilities, and the American congregation is likewise tempted to believe that it can get the job done for God if it can build up its members' confidence in the power of numbers, the hidden resources of the human spirit, and the possibilities of a determined will.

Some congregations have fallen prey to this temptation. In their desperate search to create new and effective ways to disciple men, they have lost that necessary sense of dependence upon God for all things, including the fulfillment of His commands. The problem with such congregations is not ignorance of God's purposes, but ignorance of their own inadequacy when they seek to fulfill His purposes without depending upon His power. The latter ignorance is as harmful as the former, for both deprive congregations of the kind of spiritual power God wants them to enjoy.

These problems are not new. Some of the churches addressed in the first three chapters of Revelation had reached varying degrees of spiritual dryness. Sardis had the appearance of life, but in the judgment of the Lord it was a dead congregation. Behind its busy facade, behind its reputation, behind its appearance of success, there was emptiness. Laodicea was content to dabble in a mild religion but was spiritually inert, demonstrating how dangerously easy it is to deal with the religion academically, to approach sound doctrine theoretically (even legalistically), to lapse into formal but lifeless orthodoxy, or to carry out functions habitually without being in the channel of God's activity.

Some Christians, in their dissatisfaction with the level of vitality they perceive in their congregations, have been susceptible to an inrush of dubious doctrine and practice. How much better if they would become authentically purposeful, and gain an involvement with God that is both valid and satisfying.

How Congregations Can Regain
Spiritual Power

What can be done to remove hindrances to spiritual power? How can congregations achieve results greater than mere human effort could ever produce? The answer may sound simplistic, but it is entirely valid: serious Bible study and prayer must occupy a position of high priority in the congregation and in the lives of its people.

Through Bible study, Christians perceive God's purposes more clearly. They confront the need for the lost to be brought to Christ and for Christians to build up one another in the faith. They progress to greater depths of faith in God and venture forth in pursuit of His purposes, regardless of how inadequate they may feel, trusting that God will give them the strength they need. They appropriate more firmly the fact that the church, as the body of Christ, is God's primary channel for accomplishing His will in the world and that God intends for them, as members of that body, to be actively yielded instruments through which He can work. And they develop the conviction that, above all else, they must look to Him to empower them for the challenge. When they regularly read and study the Word of God, Christians begin to pursue God's purposes actively—not with a sense of a self-sufficiency, but in an attitude of dependence upon Him.

Prayer, too, is extremely important in the development of spiritual energies in a congregation. Prayer is "the nerve that moves the muscle of God's might." If Christians would see their congregations operate at optimum effectiveness in making disciples, they must not only work to that end but also pray for God's blessing in the conversion of sinners and the spiritual growth of saints.

> Without consistent prayer, we operate on our own resources and soon find our spiritual reserves depleted. Paderewski, the great Polish pianist, used to say that if he stopped practicing for one day he noticed it. If he stopped practicing for two days, his family noticed it. If he stopped for three days, the public could tell the difference. If one stops practicing the presence of God in prayer regularly, he finds his heart becoming cool, his spirit insensitive to the words of those about him, the wells of his compassion drying up, the urgency of his mission in the world subsiding.[18]

God has ordained a partnership between Christians and himself in fulfilling His aims—Christians laboring at the tasks and God enabling them to succeed. Christians grow toward the goal of God's design for their lives as (1) they strive to incorporate Christ's ways, (2) the church nurtures them, and (3) God strengthens them with power through His Spirit in their inner beings.[19]

A mental image of the church commonly held by Christians seems to be one of defense and security. The enemy is on the offensive, raging against God's people, seeking their defeat; but the church is secure within God's fortress. The walls and gates of God's defense are comforting assurances; the church is safe.

A more appropriate image is the church aggressively pursuing the victory. The enemy is the one who retreats and seeks security because God provides the armor and weapons for His people. Paul exhorts Christians to "put on the full armor" that God has provided, in order that His people might be fully prepared to win the victory.[20] The warfare-victory motif figures prominently in the apostle's letters:

> For though we live in the world, we do not wage war as the world does. The weapons we fight with are not the weapons of the world. On the contrary, they have divine power to demolish strongholds.[21]

There is no need to wait, as Jesus told His apostles to do. Pentecost has already come. The Spirit has been given. The power is available. It is God now who sometimes must wait for His people to tap into that power in the pursuit of His goals.

The church need not timidly shrink back, apologize, harbor uncertainty, or be afraid. It cannot fail if it seeks what God is seeking, if it has joined God in His cause. It is Christ's ambassador, backed up by the resources of Heaven. It can, in confidence, launch undertakings that by human estimate would be impossible.

Paul wrote, "I can do everything through him who gives me strength."[22]

For Further Reading

McGavran, Donald, and George Hunter. *Church Growth Strategies That Work.* Nashville: Abingdon, 1980.

Peters, George W. *A Theology of Church Growth.* Grand Rapids: Zondervan, 1981.

Schaeffer, Francis A. *The Church at the End of the 20th Century.* Downers Grove, IL: Inter-Varsity, 1970.

————— *True Spirituality.* Wheaton, IL: Tyndale House Publishers, 1977.

Stedman, Ray. *Authentic Christianity*. Waco, TX: Word, 1975.

Tippett, Alan. *Church Growth and the Word of God*. Grand Rapids: Eerdmans, 1970.

Wagner, C. Peter. *Your Church Can Grow*. Glendale: Regal, 1976.

---

[1]Ephesians 1:3, 4

[2]Acts 2:22-47; Hebrews 8, 9

[3]Acts 2

[4]Matthew 28:18-20

[5]Mark 16:20

[6]Acts 1:4, 8

[7]R.E.O. White, *Five Minutes with the Master* (Grand Rapids: Eerdmans, 1965), p. 147.

[8]1 Corinthians 3:6-9

[9]Colossians 2:19

[10]Romans 12:6-8; 1 Corinthians 12:4-31

[11]Romans 1:16

[12]1 Thessalonians 1:5

[13]1 Corinthians 2:3-5

[14]Luke 19:26

[15]Ray C. Stedman, *Authentic Christianity* (Waco, TX: Word Books, 1975), p. 75.

[16]Donald A. McGavran, *How Churches Grow* (New York: Friendship Press, 1965), p. 56.

[17]A. R. Tippett, *Church Growth and the Word of God* (Grand Rapids: Eerdmans, 1970), pp. 50, 51.

[18]Robert A. Raines, *New Life in the Church* (New York: Harper & Row, 1961), p. 60.

[19]Ephesians 3:16-20; Romans 8:26, 27

[20]Ephesians 6:10-17

[21]2 Corinthians 10:3, 4

[22]Philippians 4:13

Part Three

PROBLEMS THAT HINDER PURPOSE

Section Outline

7. *Reversal of Means and Ends*
   A. Routine
   B. Traditionalism
   C. Institutionalism

8. *Cultural Distortion*
   A. Distortions of Purpose
   B. Distortions of Commitment
   C. Distortions of Ministry
   D. Distortions of Outreach
   E. Other Distortions

9. *Personal Dynamics*
   A. Incentive Systems
   B. Means-Ends Commitments
   C. Interpersonal Relations

Christians are sometimes baffled by discrepancies between what the church ought to be and what it is. The purposes that really operate in churches are not always the ones we assume, not necessarily those we profess.

God's purposes and objectives sometimes remain only as figureheads, legitimizing the existence of the congregation but exerting little actual influence on its life and work. In order to know the real purposes at work in a congregation, it might be necessary to reason backward from programs and practices to see what they are tending to accomplish. When church people undertake such an examination, they are often surprised to discover that very little of their efforts is contributing to discipling the world through evangelism and nurture.

Christians tend to assume that the sociologist will be puzzled when he tries to analyze a Christian congregation. They assume the church will not fit any of his models; while he deals with *organizations,* the church is an *organism* of a type not found anywhere else in the world. Yet in many ways the church is well described by sociological theories—at least in the short view and in a given time and place—because organisms must have organization in order to live and function. The church is an organism, but it has organizational and institutional characteristics, and in these characteristics exists the potential for undermining purpose.

Christians have sometimes assumed that the church can only be understood theologically. But while a valid theology of the church is imperative, it leaves unsolved some of the puzzles encountered in congregations. Theology deals with the divine and ideal nature of the church, while many of the existing contradictions arise from the fact that human beings make up the church, giving rise to sociological processes.

Students of organizations tend to be pessimistic, since their observations indicate that institutions have within them the seeds of their own destruction. Organizations seem doomed to follow patterns that will eventually render them ineffective. But this is where the sociologists' theories fall short, for the church does not grow old and permanently ineffective as do other organizations. It has within it a life that will not be quenched. It contains at all times the seeds of rebirth, as history has repeatedly demonstrated.

After two decades of ministry in local churches, I engaged in a program of study at a major university. In a section of courses on the sociology of organizations, I gained insights into congregational characteristics which had puzzled and sometimes frustrated me. I found that the gap between what is and what ought to be often arises from processes common to most institutions. These processes tend to operate in congregations the same as they do in other settings involving human interaction. The insights which grew out of the study enabled me to work more intelligently to solve some of the problems with which I grappled. Other difficulties which could not be solved immediately were more tolerable because at least I understood what they were. Certain processes were no longer mysterious; they had names and could be identified; other people dealt with them, too.

The purpose of the following chapters is to provide diagnostic insight into the origin of certain problems common to churches so that leaders may help their congregations cope with the problems in order to achieve Christ's purpose more effectively. The processes that tend to undermine purpose fall into three major classifications: a reversal of means and ends, cultural distortions, and personal dynamics.

7

Reversal of
Means and Ends

As you read, think about these questions:
—Why do institutions sometimes fail to pursue their legitimate purposes as clearly and productively as they should?
—How do means and ends become confused by those who are trying to achieve God's purpose?
—What are the values and dangers of routine? Of tradition?
—What is institutionalism? How does it tend to hinder churches?

A church consultant had the following experience during a study with an old, prestigious congregation. In the immediate vicinity of the church building he found scores of children who were receiving no Christian influence or instruction but who expressed eagerness to be taught. The consultant went to a large Sunday-school class of men and explained the opportunity. He offered to recruit classes of these youngsters and help some of the men begin teaching them.

The proposal was rejected, because the men's class was in an attendance contest with a women's class, and would surely lose if some of the men left to teach the children.

Coleridge wrote of truths that are considered so unquestionably true that we put them to bed in the dormitory of the soul, where they lose all power of truth. Purposes are extremely vulnerable to this fate. The more obvious they are, the more likely they are to be taken for granted and lose the power to give direction to action. The book of Hebrews warns Christians: "We must pay more careful attention, therefore, to what we have heard, so that we do not drift away."[1]

Sometimes churches do drift away, and lose sight of God's purpose, devoting their energies instead to the various means they designed in order to achieve it.

Organizations and their leaders deal with two categories of concerns: means and ends. *Ends* are the ultimate objectives, goals, or purposes that an organization is supposed to achieve. *Means* are the tools, the instrumental concerns that help to accomplish the ends. In the church, the God-given ends are evangelizing the lost and restoring the saved to God's design for living. The means for accomplishing these ends are many. Some of the means are divinely stipulated, such as preaching, teaching, baptizing, fellowship, worship, and pastoral oversight. Other means are expedient—they are devised by the church for a given time and place. Expedient means commonly employed by congregations today include Sunday schools, youth groups, newsletters, committees, study groups, shepherding groups, audiovisual aids, literature, calling programs, retreats, revivals, camps, missionary enterprises, and educational institutions.

In organizations of all kinds, attention persistently tends to shift from ends to means in such a way that the ends are neglected. This tendency is so prevalent and so strong that some students of organizations consider the process almost inevitable. The process is readily observable in businesses, industries, educational enterprises, social organizations, governments and their structures—and in the church.

Systems of thought and action tend to become closed, narrowing and shortening vision, smothering creativity, and rewarding routine. Bureaucracies are notable for trapping their employees in unexamined and often illogical application of rules and procedures. The philosopher Nietzsche observed that many people are stubborn in pursuit of the path they have chosen, but few in pursuit of their goal. Practices that once were deliberate means to important ends soon come to be expected and carried out for their own sakes. Perpetuating them becomes an end in itself, while the original purpose is displaced.

In the church this reversal occurs as attention is drawn from God's purposes to routines, activities, forms, traditions, and institutional concerns.

Routine

Routine can settle in almost imperceptibly, in such a way that God's purpose for His church is assumed and therefore neglected.

Ineffectiveness occurs more often by default than by intention. Simple neglect can be deadly to the achievement of objectives. Means, once developed in order to achieve desired ends, solidify into expectations, entrench into precedents, and become sacrosanct through sheer repetition. Unless the church can ward off such processes, its vital qualities may deteriorate:

Organism, into organization;
community, into association;
mission orientation, into maintenance orientation;
fellowship, into formality;
function, into form;
success-seeking, into survival-seeking;
pursuit of accomplishment, into pursuit of convenience;
discipleship, into churchmanship;
the work of the church, into church work;
leadership, into bureaucracy;
team members, into spectators or clients;
purpose, into routine.

Unless a congregation maintains a purposeful attitude toward every activity, it may decline into a weary perpetuator of motions. The meetings may go on, and the doors of the building stay open, but nothing happens—or is expected to happen. Staying in existence and preserving familiar means may become the goal, while meaning and purpose fade into oblivion.

Habit has its value. Once effectiveness procedures are established, time and effort are conserved. But procedures must be constantly evaluated and continued deliberately for only as long as they are, in fact, effective. Maintaining practices by default, rather than by intention, is deadening.

The Activity Trap

In addition to thoughtless routine, means may replace ends if people focus attention or concern upon activities themselves rather than upon the outcome the activities are to produce. This phenomenon has been called "the activity trap" (carrying out the activity becomes of prime importance, to the neglect of goals) and "program orientation" (the imperative is the next program, with little sense of the objectives to be accomplished through that program).

We tend to confuse busyness with effectiveness. As long as the wheels are spinning, committees are meeting, and people are rushing here and there, we feel confident something must be getting done. The activity fallacy can be illustrated by the man who collected all kinds of junk and fitted it together in his barn. A wonderful machine evolved. Wheels turned, gears meshed, pulleys pulled, lights flashed, bells rang, and buzzers buzzed. The only problem was that the machine did not do anything; it just ran. Then there was the fabled axle grease factory that consumed all its product just to keep its own machinery lubricated; nothing came off the production line.

In the business world, focusing upon an activity rather than upon appropriate ends has been called "marketing myopia." When highway and air transportation became possible, most railroad companies already in existence did not develop truck lines, bus lines, and airlines, although this would have seemed natural. Many of these companies thought of themselves as in the railroading activity and continued to think this way. This focus upon one kind of activity serves as a mental block, shutting out opportunities for growth or expansion. New companies had to come into existence to develop the new means of transportation. But a few railroad companies thought of themselves as in the transportation business which, incidentally, had used railroading as a means up to that time. Such companies were alert to new means because their mindset was not locked into the existing means. This same phenomenon can be observed in many areas of enterprise.

The difference between a "means" orientation and an "ends" orientation may be seen in the self-description of an aged preacher. As a young man in his first ministry he found himself each Sunday morning walking reluctantly to the church building, dreading the ordeal of the pulpit. The typical prayer of his leaden heart was, "Lord, let the building burn down before I have to try to preach this sermon." After years of experience, he came to his last ministry with a far different attitude. His Sunday morning prayer became, "Lord, if that building is going to burn down, don't let it happen until after I have preached this sermon." The difference, as he described it, was this: "On the first occasion, I had to preach a sermon; in the last, I had a sermon to preach." He had reversed his focus from the means he had to carry out to the end he fervently wanted to accomplish through the sermon.

For a drama company, the performance on the stage is the end to be achieved. The event itself is the goal. For such Christian activities as preaching, teaching, or worship, the event itself is not the end to be achieved, it is the means. The goal must be that of accomplishing God's will in the church and in the lives of people through the particular activity.

Formalism

Purpose prescribes certain functions. Forms, in turn, are developed to provide for the functions. In other words, form follows function, and both are dictated by purpose. God did not incidentally create the configuration of the human hand and then try to find a use for it—He created man, according to His purposes, to perform certain functions. Some of those functions are best carried out by the physiological form that we call a hand.

Formalism, however, focuses upon forms themselves—so intently that the related function and the ultimate purpose may be neglected. In the church, expedient practices, programs, procedures, and building styles are sometimes handed down as established forms that are far from suited to functions. It is frequently a challenge to find ways to function within these forms in order to fulfill, in some measure, the real purpose of the church.

Formalism can even focus upon a divinely stipulated form in such a way that the purpose behind it is hindered or lost. The religious formalists of Jesus' day were so nearsighted about their pet forms that they failed to be concerned about the "weightier matters" of judgment, mercy, and faith.[2] The Pharisees were Biblical legalists but they were not committed to God's purposes and priorities. They were experts at form, able to argue skillfully matters of "jots and tittles."[3] Their theology was neatly systematized. But they focused on forms to the extent that they not only lost sight of God's intentions, but worked against them.[4] Legalists frequently seek more to control others' thought and practice than to promote the accomplishment of God's objectives. The ability to argue issues of doctrine to final conclusions is no substitute for implementing the intentions of God.

Some Christians appear to think that the idea is equivalent to the deed. When we sing hymns, for example, we sometimes make extravagant affirmations and commitments that we do not actually intend to carry out. Expressing the idea is its own end, and the intention of implementing it is not seriously entertained. For this reason neither speakers nor hearers seriously anticipate life-transforming application of much that is preached and taught. Saying and hearing the idea is substituted for the deed.

It is possible for a church to perceive itself as strongly Biblical and yet be static, to espouse the Great Commission and yet not implement it seriously, to affirm Christ as Lord and yet not incorporate His principles into life.

Forms are important; those that are divinely established are imperative. God's forms must be followed, and expedient forms must be carefully chosen, but both must be followed in such a deliberate way that the essential purposes are fulfilled through them. To concentrate on the form while neglecting its purpose is to misuse any form. The church cannot assume it is functioning as God intended simply because it believes its forms are in correct order. No doctrinal position is adequate that does not include an *operating* commitment to the pursuit of God's purposes.

Traditionalism

In the title of one of his books, Ralph Neighbour summed up the problem of tradition becoming more important than accomplishing the real goal of the church. He called the book, *The Seven Last Words of the Church: We Never Tried It That Way Before.*

Traditionalism goes a step beyond routine or formalism. Traditionalism elevates expedient forms or practices to a sacrosanct position and *insists* upon their perpetuation.

As traditions become sacrosanct they move outside the realm of question or examination. They collect loyalties, psychological investments, and commitments, so that in the minds of people their perpetuation becomes imperative. A military officer once remarked that he felt more personal danger trying to change procedures in the Pentagon than on the battlefields of Vietnam.

Christians and churches often continue certain patterns, not because there is any reason for it in Biblical Christianity, but because down through history someone started doing things that way and the practice stuck. We hold ideas and attitudes in the same way, and woe to the person who questions them or suggests a change!

A look at some of the characteristics of traditions will show how greatly they can affect the functions of the church.

Traditions form quickly. A banquet was in progress in a brand new hotel. The building, of bold and innovative design, was not yet completed, but portions were in use. During the salad course of the banquet, one of the guests asked a waiter for crackers. Recoiling visibly, the waiter retorted, "Sir, it is not the tradition of this hotel to serve crackers." In a building not yet finished, traditions were already entrenched.

In the day-to-day life of any organization, decisions are made, practices are initiated, and directions are established that almost immediately become traditions. It is astonishing how rapidly traditions develop and how rigid they can become.

Traditions frequently outlive any semblance of reason. When Bismarck of Germany was making an official call on the Czar of Russia, he noticed a guard standing, for no apparent reason, in the middle of the lawn. Bismarck inquired about the reason for the sentry. The Czar admitted he did not know why, but for as long as he could remember, guards had stood at that spot twenty-four hours a day. The Czar questioned other members of the staff about the tradition. No one knew the reason for it. The captain of the guard, finally, was able to discover the reason.

Several decades before, the Czar's grandmother had noticed a wild flower blooming at that spot in the lawn and ordered a guard posted to keep careless feet from trampling it. The little flower was long since gone, but no one rescinded the order; no one questioned the tradition. Two generations later, sentries were still being posted at the spot, twenty-four hours a day, seven days a week, fifty-two weeks a year—for no reason whatever.

"Bureaucracy defends the status quo long past the time when the quo has lost its status."[5]

Traditions may become handicaps. In the jungles of South

America, anthropologists found a tribe of people living in huts built atop tall platforms. They asked why the huts were constructed that way, but the natives thought the question ridiculous. The natives admitted their houses were somewhat inconvenient—but that's the way life is, and that's the way houses are built, so why raise foolish questions? As the anthropologists probed the history of the tribe, they discovered that several generations before, the people had been lake dwellers and fishermen. Now the question was answered. There is a reason for building a house on poles, if the house is in a lake. The tradition of building houses in that fashion had become sacrosanct, so when changing circumstances forced the tribe to move into the jungles and become hunters, they did not question their traditional way of building houses. They simply continued the custom even though it no longer served any purpose and was now, in fact, a handicap.

The programs and practices in today's congregations must be constantly open to examination to insure they are productive of the commissioned purpose. Some may be irrelevant to committed discipleship. Some may be out-and-out hindrances.

Traditions may blind us to opportunities and shut out improvements. One student of churches tells of talking with a farmer not far from a large city. The farmer, who had been a lifelong participant in his congregation, sadly remarked that the future of that congregation did not seem promising. The church was doomed to decline, he said, unless farm people would start moving back into the area, and that was not likely to happen with so many housing developments taking over the farmland in all directions. Here was a church so caught in its own traditional self-image that it could not see the developing of new and vast opportunities for fulfilling God's purpose.

We flounder sometimes in the quicksand of traditional attitudes, expectation, and habits. Who can guess how we limit ourselves and the kingdom of God by our invalid assumptions? Jesus pointed out that the religionists of His day were so busy following the details of their traditions and seeing that others did the same, they had abandoned the commands of God.[6] They were, in fact, working contrary to God's objectives. Jesus had a difficult time changing people's thinking about the kingdom of God. Their errors were so firmly planted in their traditions, they could not understand the truth Jesus brought. One of the earliest problems in the church was the difficulty that some people (the Judaizers) had letting go their former religious traditions in order to follow Jesus.

Sometimes man is prone even to confuse his traditions with the will of God. He is often unwilling or unable to distinguish between expedients developed during the history of the church and principles laid down in Scripture, and this inability hinders the church from discipling the world.

A word must be said about an equal and opposite error. Some people are impatient with all existing practices, willing to discard them without serious evaluation and adopt whatever is new at the moment. They think that change—any change—will be an improvement. Such an attitude may be no more purposeful than thoughtlessly perpetuating routine. Ineffective new ways are no better than ineffective old ways. People who constantly tinker with procedures should consider the wisdom in the motto: "If it ain't broke, don't fix it." The secret to effectiveness, may not be in discovering new ways of doing things but in keeping the meaning alive in existing ways.

Like habits, traditions may be harmless, or they may even be genuinely productive of purpose. Traditionalism, however, insists upon maintaining the tradition even if it is counterproductive. Traditions must be subject to two conditions: (1) They must be recognized as traditions and not confused with the mandates of God; and (2) maintaining them must contribute to, not interfere with, accomplishing God's purposes.

W. Carl Ketcherside has dealt clearly with the problem of traditionalism in today's churches:

> "We're all so clogged with dead ideas passed from generation to generation that even the best of us don't know the way out."—Peter Weiss, Marat/Sade.
>
> One who challenges the traditions of a people must always be prepared to face their hostility. When opinions have become crystallized by constant repetition men are frightened at the thought of divesting themselves of them. Wtihout them they feel helpless and insecure. They regard the surrender of them as being an unfair reflection upon their fathers, and fear that a denial of them will weaken the truth which they have sought to buttress with them.
>
> It was Thomas Carlyle, the Scottish essayist and historian, who wrote, "What an enormous magnifier is tradition? How a thing grows in the human memory and in the human imagination, when love, worship, and all that is in the human heart, is there to encourage it."

I am not by nature an iconoclast, an idol-smasher. I think a lot of traditions are harmless and insignificant and I have no ambition to go around slashing at them for the mere satisfaction of revealing them for what they are. But others are detrimental to the revealed truth of heaven, because they parade as truth, and many contribute to the destruction of souls. I am an avowed enemy of anything which obstructs the eternal purpose.

In the Hall of Fame for Great Americans at New York University is a bust of Mark Twain. Beneath it are the words, "Loyalty to petrified opinion never yet broke a chain or freed a human soul." I am resolved with the help of God to stand by, with, and for the truth of heaven, but I feel no compulsion to defend with equal fervor those traditions which are "ours." I say this despite the fact that Thomas Babington Macaulay wrote, "To almost all men the state of things under which they have been used to live seems to be the necessary state of things."[7]

Institutionalism

If a visitor from another planet were to visit some of our churches and attend the board meetings, read the church papers, and listen to the conversations, he might conclude that the purposes of the church are: to increase membership, balance the budget, have a bigger Sunday school than the church down the street, make an impression on the brotherhood, keep up the property, build a new building, and carry adequate insurance on the facilities. This particular variety of means-ends reversal occurs when the care of the institution becomes the major concern.

Whenever people by design communicate with each other more than once about a common concern or function together in an arranged way, they have an institution. If two businessmen meet by accident, have coffee, and talk over business they do not have an institution. But if they find the experience worthwhile and decide to repeat it every Tuesday at ten o'clock, they have established an institution. If known people are involved in an activity at a known time and place, they have an institution, even though it may be simple.

The local congregation is an institution; at least, it has unavoidable institutional characteristics. A noninstitutional church is a contradiction in terms. One might as well speak of a nonrelated family or a nonmanufactured machine. The institutional aspects of the church are necessary. They set the church in order and help it function. But when "care and feeding" of the institution becomes more imperative than the purpose for which the church was established, problems arise. Success, maintenance, or survival of the institution itself gets in the way of accomplishing its job.

Excessive concern for institutional considerations may be seen in schools, hospitals, businesses, and most other organizations, as well as churches. Laurence Peter, for example, tells us how teachers in public schools are pressured into mediocrity so that students will not make such strides in learning that they do not fit well into the orderly progression of grade levels.[8] Nor is it unusual to find various organizations such as charitable foundations spending more than 90% of their resources on institutional processes and less than 10% on the task for which they were organized. Most institutions have their counterparts of a saying sometimes heard around hospitals: "We could run this hospital properly if it weren't for the patients."

The Jewish nation, whose development is traced in the Old Testament, is itself an example. It was a means to an end—the end being the coming of the Messiah into the world. Yet the leaders of the nation plotted to destroy the Messiah to preserve their national institution. Jesus had raised Lazarus from the dead, a demonstration of His deity, and the people were beginning to move in His direction. Some of the leaders, however, saw this only as a threat:

> Then the chief priests and the Pharisees called a meeting of the Sanhedrin, "What are we accomplishing?" they asked. "Here is this man performing many miraculous signs. If we let him go on like this, everyone will believe in him, and then the Romans will come and take away both our place and our nation." Then one of them, named Caiaphas, who was high priest that year, spoke up, "You know nothing at all! You do not realize that it is better for you that one man die for the people than that the whole nation perish." . . . So from that day on they plotted to take his life.[9]

In the church, concern for institutional aspects sometimes displaces its reason for existence. The institution then exists primarily for itself. Even something as vital to the church as its educational system is not immune to this tendency. Who could find fault with a big Sunday school? The more people being taught, the better. But something has gone wrong if, as the minister of one of the largest congregations in America charged a few years ago, some of the ten largest Sunday schools were inflating their attendance figures to stay in the "Top 10."

When institutional ideals matter more to a church than God's purpose, the criteria for success and failure are changed. In one instance, a Sunday-school teacher said he was going to quit teaching because he felt like a failure. As soon as he built attendance to the point he could meet goals set for him by the Sunday-school administration, they would take some of his students to be teachers elsewhere. Most people would say he was achieving a high degree of success, since he taught so well that his students became teachers. By institutional criteria, however, he was failing.

If we dare face it, even some of our efforts to reach other people may actually be recruitment programs in which we have the institution's need for support in mind more than the people's need for Christ. Albert Camus accused the church of offering to introduce us to God, but when we accept, we discover all that is left at the royal court is buildings, budgets, organizations, and promotion—the King is not there.

A parable by Theodore Wedel vividly portrays the church focusing upon itself while it abandons its true objectives.

On a dangerous seacoast where shipwrecks often occur there was once a crude little lifesaving station. The building was just a hut, and there was only one boat, but the few devoted members kept a constant watch over the sea, and with no thought for themselves went out day and night tirelessly searching for the lost. Many lives were saved by this wonderful little station, so that it became famous. Some of those who were saved, and various others in the surrounding area wanted to become associated with the station and give of their time and money and effort for the support of its work. New boats were bought and new crews trained. The little lifesaving station grew.

Some of the members of the lifesaving station were unhappy that the building was so crude and poorly equipped. They felt that a more comfortable place should be provided as the first refuge of those saved from the sea. So they replaced the emergency cots with beds and put better furniture in the enlarged building. Now the lifesaving station became a popular gathering place for its members, and they decorated it beautifully and furnished it exquisitely, because they used it as a sort of club. Fewer members were now interested in going to sea on lifesaving missions, so they hired lifeboat crews to do this work. The lifesaving motif still prevailed in the club's decoration, and there was a liturgical lifeboat in the room where the club initiations were held. About this time a large ship was wrecked off the coast, and the hired crews brought in boatloads of cold, wet, and half-drowned people. They were dirty and sick, and some of them had black skin and some had yellow skin. The beautiful new club was in chaos. So the property committee immediately had a shower house built outside the club where victims of the shipwreck could be cleaned up before coming inside.

At the next meeting, there was a split in the club membership. Most of the members wanted to stop the club's lifesaving activities as being unpleasant and a hindrance to the normal social life of the club. Some members insisted upon lifesaving as their primary purpose and pointed out that they were still called a lifesaving station. But they were finally voted down and told that if they wanted to save the lives of all the various kinds of people who were shipwrecked in those waters, they could begin their own lifesaving station down the coast. They did.

As the years went by, the new station experienced the same changes that had occurred in the old. It evolved into a club, and yet another lifesaving station was founded. History continued to repeat itself, and if you visit that seacoast today, you will find a number of exclusive clubs along that shore. Shipwrecks are frequent in those waters, but most of the people drown![10]

In similar fashion institutionalism brings disease to a congregation, so that its effectiveness levels off and declines. Purpose can be allowed to drown (along with the unevangelized) in a sea of institutional concerns.

All organizations must be maintained. Communications, relationships, morale, and the like must be kept in good working order. The organization must continue and be healthy if it is to accomplish its task. But it also must accomplish the task, or, ultimately, it cannot be healthy.

Maintenance is a necessary but greedy function and will take over unless guarded carefully. When institutionalism is in control, the following conditions tend to prevail:

Morale is difficult to muster and maintain, since it is linked to inadequate goals.

Criteria for selecting and evaluating officers are inappropriate.

Criteria for planning and evaluating programs or activities are flawed.

Conflict of interest and dissatisfaction with leadership are prevalent.

The law of indirection applies to institutions. The church

that sets out to build itself into a great institution may achieve a measure of success according to its own standards. The pathetic relics of once powerful religious institutions warn of the futility of this approach. Other congregations commit themselves to getting Jesus' work done and labor hard at the task. One day they look up and discover they have become great churches.

We may apply to churches what Jesus said about individuals: "For whoever wants to save his life will lose it, but whoever loses his life for me and for the gospel will save it."[11] When congregations slip into maintenance or survival as their goals, they sign their death notices (even though they may continue to exist as institutions long after they have died as genuine churches). But a church that holds a clear sense of God's purpose, of its reason for being, is marked by commitment, vitality, and enthusiasm for Christ. The members work and sacrifice, new people are reached and embraced, and the congregation thrives.

For Further Reading

Anderson, James. To Come Alive! New York: Harper and Row, 1973.

Champion, Dean. The Sociology of Organizations. New York: McGraw-Hill, 1975.

Culbert, Samuel. The Organization Trap and How to Get Out of It. New York: Basic Books, 1974.

Edge, Findley. A Quest for Vitality in Religion. Nashville: Broadman Press, 1963.

————. The Greening of the Church. Waco, Texas: Word Books, 1971.

Engle, James F. and Norton H. Wilbert. What's Gone Wrong With the Harvest? Grand Rapids: Zondervan, 1975.

Getz, Gene. Sharpening the Focus of the Church. Chicago: Moody Press, 1974.

Green, Hollis L. Why Churches Die. Minneapolis: Bethany Fellowship, 1972.

Griffith, Michael. God's Forgetful Pilgrims. Grand Rapids: Eerdmans, 1975.

Haas, Eugene. Complex Organizations: A Sociological Perspective. New York: Macmillan, 1973.

Halverson, Richard. How I Changed My Thinking About the Church. Grand Rapids: Zondervan, 1972.

Hersey, Paul. Management of Organizational Behavior. Englewood Cliffs, New Jersey: Prentice Hall, 1972.

Levinson, Harry. Organizational Diagnosis. Cambridge, Massachusetts: Harvard University, 1972.

Lindgren, Alvin and Norman Shawchuck. Management for Your Church. Nashville: Abingdon, 1977.

Merton, Robert K. et. al. Reader in Bureaucracy. New York Free Press, 1952.

Metz, Donald. New Congregations: Security and Mission in Conflict. New York: Westminster Press, 1967.

Montgomery, John Warwick. Damned Through the Church. Minneapolis: Bethany Fellowship, 1970.

Peter, Laurence J. The Peter Principle. New York: Bantam Books, 1969.
_____. The Peter Prescription. New York: Bantam Books, 1972.

Richards, Larry. A New Face for the Church. Grand Rapids: Zondervan, 1970.

Schaller, Lyle E. Hey, That's Our Church. Nashville: Abingdon, 1975.

Schuller, Robert. Your Church Has Real Possibilities. Glendale: Regal, 1974.

Thompson, James D. Organizations in Action. New York: McGraw-Hill, 1967.

Wagner, C. Peter. Your Church Can Grow. Glendale: Regal, 1976.

---

¹Hebrews 2:1

²Matthew 23:23-32

³Matthew 5:18

⁴Matthew 23:1-39

⁵Laurence J. Peter, The Peter Prescription. (New York: Bantam Books, 1972), p. 18.

⁶Mark 7:1-13

⁷W. Carl Ketcherside, Mission Messenger. (Volume 35, Number 7, July, 1973). Used by permission.

⁸Laurence J. Peter, The Peter Principle. (New York: Bantam Books, 1969), p. 26.

⁹John 11:47-53

¹⁰This paraphrase by Richard Wheatcroft appeared in Howard Clinebell's Basic Types of Pastoral Counseling (New York: Abingdon, 1966), pp. 13, 14.

¹¹Mark 8:35

8

Cultural Distortion

As you read, think about these questions:
—How does our culture look upon church membership?
—How does our culture look upon the church's role in the world?
—How has culture changed the Biblical ideals of stewardship, ministry, fellowship, and commitment?
—How can differences between a congregation and its cultural setting impede the transmission of the gospel?

Western culture is replete with stereotypes of the church—what it is, what its role is supposed to be in the world, how it is to behave toward the rest of society, how it is expected to function, what it should teach, how it should conduct worship, how it should (or should not!) evangelize, what its buildings should look like, what a good sermon is, and what should be done at such events as weddings and funerals. It establishes roles and norms for ministers, officers, and members.

More than Christians sometimes realize, they are influenced in their assumptions about the church by cultural expectations.

From the time an individual is born, culture filters into him its assumptions about the church. Even before he is aware of what is happening, the cultural image is well-structured into his thinking, so that he tends to accept and perpetuate what he has heard and observed. The cultural versions of religion resemble Christianity in many ways and use some of the same terminology and forms, but they lack the essence of Biblical Christianity. If congregations are not alert, they can be directed more by culture's image of Christianity than by what the Bible reveals as the intentions of God. This condition has been described as the "cultural captivity of the church."

From the very beginning of Christianity, the church was in danger of altering its God-given intentions because of cultural pressures. Tendencies emerged to change the doctrines of Christ and to separate Christians into argumentative groups. Some people wanted to mix the ideas and practices of Judaism with Christianity. Others tended to import pagan philosophies and customs. Still others simply misunderstood some aspects of Christianity. During the lifetimes of the apostles, such tendencies were held in check. The New Testament letters show how the apostles held Christianity to its original character.

After the apostles died, movements toward deviation progressed more rapidly. One generation would make alterations in doctrine or practice. The next generation would accept the changes without question and add some of their own. Over a period of several generations, the changes became extreme, elements of paganism sifted in, and the church delved into political alliances.

At times (as church history extensively documents), society has tried to adopt the church as one of its institutions, neutralizing its impact or bending its influence to serve social ends. At other times, culture has developed a kind of "folk religion" version of the church out of a failure to understand Biblical Christianity.

Through such processes, culture frequently subverts the purpose and nature of the church. It fosters in people characteristics that profoundly affect (often negatively) the way they function as Christians. It dampens purposefulness and militancy in congregations, encumbers Christianity with unproductive traditions, and undermines the vigorous pursuit of Christ's Commission.

Distortions of Purpose

Cultural stereotypes of Christianity are usually weaker in purpose than the New Testament intends. Biblical norms are "taken with a grain of salt." "Surely," says the stereotype, "those standards are not to be taken seriously—they are over-statements that have to be diluted to a practical level. A comfortable truce between the church and the world is preferable to a state of tension. Joining the church can't be as radical as Scripture seems to indicate following Jesus is supposed to be. No one can expect that much! Adding church membership to an otherwise 'normal' life is a much more realistic way to live than getting carried away with extreme ideas."

One church member described an all too prevalent condition. He had, in his words, "oozed into" conventional church membership. He had grown up attending Sunday school and various other church functions. At one point in his youth he realized he was expected to do something about church membership, so he carried out the prescribed procedures. But he had never seriously decided to be a disciple of Jesus, nor had he given Jesus the role of Lord in his life. He had merely added church membership to an otherwise unchanged life.

Not only does culture tend to dilute God's purposes: cultural images of the church often have quite different purposes than the church of the New Testament. Such purposes range all the way from innocuous generalizations to the support of esthetic, social, or political goals.

Religious institutions sometimes become patrons of the arts, promoting fine music, drama, architecture, and the like.

Sometimes churches embrace social objectives in support of the current establishment. Tom Skinner has suggested that a theology has been developed to support an Americanized cultural expression of religion. "John the Baptist," he says, "has become the chaplain in Herod's palace."

In other cases churches are recruited into crusades for social reform. Christians, of course, must be concerned about the distresses of people in the world,[1] about moral, political, and economic issues of the society in which they live. Many Christians and churches have been negligent of such matters. Yet the church must guard against being swept along by social forces to the neglect of its own purpose. It must function in these concerns as the agent of God, not the agent of society. It must respond to divine imperative, not to cultural stereotype.

The weak, confused cultural image of the church stands in stark contrast to the creative tension between the church and the world in the beginning era of Christianity. Despite the hostility of society and orders to desist, the church pursued its mission. It evangelized everywhere. Its people lived like citizens of the kingdom of Heaven and, therefore, like aliens to the world. They formed themselves into congregations that were like colonies of a foreign society. Their allegiance was to Jesus Christ as Lord. They lived in this world as agents of their Lord, sent to serve His interests. When the apostles were hauled in before the court, the high priest charged, "We gave you strict orders not to teach in this name. Yet you have filled Jerusalem with your teaching."[2] What was that teaching? Anyone in Jerusalem could have told you: Jesus, crucified and raised from the dead, is Christ and Lord; therefore, repent, obey, and follow Him.

What would people today say that the church teaches, especially congregations that follow the cultural version of Christianity? "What is the church all about? What is it trying to say?" asked one uninformed man of a friend. "Oh, I'm not quite sure," said the other, "but it's something like, 'Be nice to Granny and the cat.' " Perhaps this example is a bit unfair, but some people really do believe that, because the church never taught them otherwise.

Distortions of Commitment

Commitment is essential to human life and interaction. Yet in contemporary society people are more and more unwilling to bind themselves with commitments. They are increasingly irresponsible as students, workers, citizens, marriage partners, and parents. And the penalty for such departure from divine principle is taking its toll in society and in individual lives. When this characteristic is carried over into the church, the result is devastating.

Instead of commitment, a religious consumerism prevails in cultural versions of the church. The church's energies are not directed primarily to the accomplishment of God's goals for the unreached world or His goals for the growth of His people. They are consumed in satisfying the expectations of the members as "customers." Members are the recipients of ministry, patrons of religious service. They view the church as one of the service institutions they use. Just as they are clients of hospitals and doctors for medical services, and customers of supermarkets and restaurants, they are consumers of the church's services.

Many members of churches have the attitude that the church is a kind of religious club in which they hold membership. According to their whim, they participate in its activities or stay away. The minister is looked upon as a combination "pro" and business manager whom they pay to keep the church in business for their convenience.

Americans' propensity for corporateness contributes to the problem. We are constantly transferring responsibility from individuals to some committee, agency, or board. We tend to institutionalize initiative, program functions, or organize work in such a way that personal responsibility diminishes. Passive, non-responsible individuals look to corporate entities, such as government agencies, to act *for* them and, indeed, take care *of* them. Americans as Christians are sometimes inclined to function the same way toward the church.

Not all the current movement to revive enthusiasm in the church is going in the direction of restoring Christians' commitment to God's purpose. This enthusiasm may be as self-seeking and dead-ended as the staid religion it seeks to correct. Super-spirituality can become spiritual self-gratification. Some of the Corinthians who considered themselves super-saints were unmasked in Paul's diagnosis as only spiritual infants. Heights of emotional experience is no substitute for determined, sometimes dogged, service in the cause of Christ.

The concept of *stewardship* in the Bible refers to a person entrusted with the affairs of another. Christians are entrusted with God's affairs in the world. The modern concept of stewardship in many churches, however, has subtly shifted to nothing more than the giving of money to the congregation's budget. The congregation, corporately, is deemed responsible for looking after God's affairs. Individuals simply fund these efforts, shifting their personal responsibility to the corporate shoulders.

The goals of Christianity are intended to be pursued by Christians, individually and collectively as the body of Christ. Christians should respond spontaneously to emerging opportunities in the home, the neighborhood, the community, the nation, the place of employment. And the church as a corporate entity should provide systematic, collaborative means for conducting God's affairs in the world.

Distortions of Ministry

Our culture tells us a great deal about "the minister," and much of what it says is inaccurate. It has presented an image of how he should look, what his job is, how he is to act, what he is supposed to do in times of illness and death, upon whom he is supposed to call and how often and for what occasions, and even what his family should be like. "The ministry"—that vocation in which one is overwhelmed with meetings and a myriad of tasks, torn by conflicting expectations, molded by centuries-old traditions of the pastor-priest—seems impossible to increasing numbers of candidates who sincerely yearn to serve God.

One of the most far-reaching cultural distortions of the concept of ministry began during the time of the Roman emperor Constantine. When Constantine made Christianity the official religion of the empire, he declared all citizens to be members of the church. Engulfed by masses of unconverted people, the church allowed its membership to drift into two categories— the church at large, and an elite "church within the church" composed of the clergy. The clergy carried out the functions of the church while the laity looked on and became receivers of the services of the clergy. A type of religious-political totalitarianism prevailed as the Dark Ages settled over much of western civilization. Ignorance and superstition continued to creep into the church.

Eventually, individuals began rising up to protest the conditions in the church. The Bible was given greater prominence again, especially when printing made it widely available. Leaders began the gigantic task of reform.

The reformation clearly affirmed the Scriptural principle of the priesthood of all believers. The restoration movement in America early in the nineteenth century was determined to abolish the clergy-laity distinction. Doctrine was corrected, but practice, by and large, did not keep pace. Movements of reformation have, in effect, pulled down the clergy system without fully reviving the alternative. The concept of the priesthood of all believers has served to teach Christians that they have access to God without clerical mediation, but it has not completely engaged them in service. Many who ought to be responsibly involved in achieving the purposes of Jesus Christ are inert, having been described as "God's frozen assets."[3]

In some instances the clergy system has crept back in (while being disavowed), creating an ambiguous situation in which "the minister" is a kind of hired servant of the people and always on trial depending on how his performance pleases them. It may be that the efforts at reform tended to eliminate the clergy in favor of the laity when, in fact, the concept of *laity* should have given way. All Christians should become ministers, with some of their number serving as specialized equippers of the rest.

To this day the Biblical role of the church member has not been substantially reclaimed. Christians, by and large, do not yet demonstrate a clear awareness of the demand for serious, even radical, commitment. They tend to be pale shadows of the dynamic, Spirit-filled world-changers the New Testament describes. The primary doers—those responsible for getting Christ's work done—remain the salaried ministers. Many of the church members continue to be observers of ministry, perpetuating a platform-audience relationship.

Distortions of Outreach

In addition to distortions of Scriptural concepts, culture has also imposed certain forms and trappings on Christianity that are not wrong in themselves, but impede the transmission of the gospel to other cultures.

This was the experience of one church in an ethnically changing community. The congregation had grown and flourished among people of an ethnic group that originally comprised the community. Over the course of years the original group moved to other communities and was replaced by another. For all practical purposes the entire congregation now lived in other communities and drove back in at the time of services to meet in their original building. It was a non-resident congregation, unable to evangelize the community around its building and unsuccessful at evangelizing the communities where the people now lived. They attempted to draw a nucleus of people from the area around the building and gradually develop a congregation indigenous to the present culture. The original members would then become members of congregations where they now lived. The transition was not easy, but showed promise of succeeding until a clash occurred over the type of music to be used. Some of the original members tolerated many other kinds of adjustment but adamantly refused to have "that funny music" used in worship. A European classical style used for years had become identified as "church music." Other styles of rhythm and harmony were not acceptable. By the same token, the style in use did not strike a response or sound like "church music" to the newer ethnic group.

Christianity must be true to its character and purpose, yet meaningful to the people of any given time and place. The delicate key is to avoid diluting or distorting Christianity in the process of adapting it to a given culture. Christian strategy deliberately adopts cultural forms and styles or violates them depending upon their congruence with Christianity and upon what is productive to evangelism.

McGavran points out another fact of culture that should not be overlooked. The concept of America as a melting pot of culture, he says, is a myth. America is and has always been a mosaic of many cultures. It is a plural, compound society composed of many identifiable cultures. Most ministry areas have various cultural units within them. Some cultural differences are obvious; some are subtle; but all are significant. Some writers argue for a separate congregation in each major homogeneous cultural unit. Others resist this practice on philosophical or theological grounds and appeal for a oneness in Christ that will override cultural barriers.

Whichever view a congregation chooses, it must take into account the culture of cultures of the people it seeks to evangelize if it is to function intelligently and effectively as God's agent in its particular time and place. If a congregation is to minister to more than one subgroup of society, it must be especially alert to blend styles and programs appropriate to all the cultures represented.

Other Distortions

Other essential conditions for purposeful churches have been undermined by cultural distortions. These conditions include fellowship, spiritual vitality, and the equipping of Christians to serve God's purposes.

Fellowship is redefined in cultural versions of Christianity into a much more superficial relationship than the Biblical ideal establishes. At best, the substitute relationship is one of polite, casual goodwill, but it can range all the way from indifference to competitiveness or hostility.

Spiritual vigor is also contrary to widespread cultural norms for religion. In our present cultural environment, it is socially acceptable to believe deeply and interact with God profoundly, as long as such matters are kept on a private level. But in conversation one must carefully avoid disclosing them lest he be perceived as naive, if not foolish or radical. Prayer is acceptable as long as it is general and not seriously expected to produce divine involvement in human experience. The nature and power of God are appropriate subjects for the pulpit and classroom as long as they are dealt with academically or abstractly.

American culture also sets up expectations for Christian education that often fall far short of a systematic *equipping* of people to function as the people of God. Superficial information is often the most one is expected to gain in such activities. Competence in knowledge and skill, significant personal growth, or transformation of attitudes and values are not really anticipated (or perhaps wanted) in the cultural stereotype.

The congregation that seeks to equip its people for Christian living and service, develop significant levels of fellowship, or be actively involved with God as a living presence, must be prepared to encounter the inertia of expectations deeply ingrained in social norms—and perhaps in our own thought and habit.

For Further Reading

Smart, James D. *The Cultural Subversion of the Biblical Faith.* Westminster Press.

---

[1]Matthew 25:31-46
[2]Acts 5:28
[3]Mark Gibbs and Ralph Morton. *God's Frozen People* (Philadelphia: Westminster Press, 1965).

9

Personal Dynamics

As you read, think about these questions:
— What are "incentives"? What are three types of incentives and how do they differ?
— How do types of incentive affect the way people function in organizations? Why do people with different types have difficulty understanding each other and working together?
— How do relationships among church members affect the way a congregation accomplishes its purpose?
— How does people's commitment to means or ends affect the way a congregation accomplishes its purpose?

Three types of processes threaten the role of purpose in the church. One set arises from the institutional aspects of a congregation; another set originates from inaccurate cultural images of Christianity; the third set stems from the ways persons tend to relate to institutions and to one another in social situations.

Incentive Systems[1]

People participate in organizations for different reasons or incentives. Of course, people do not logically analyze their attitudes, decide which type person they are going to be, and then act accordingly. Most people are unaware of their own tendencies. And most people have a mixture of incentives, over which one incentive predominates.

Three major kinds of incentives have been identified: material, solidary, and purposeful. An individual's relationship to an organization, especially with regard to his commitment to the means and ends of that organization, is profoundly affected by which incentive is predominant in him.

Material Incentives

Description: The person receives a material reward for being in the organization or participating in the activities. He may have no concern for the stated purpose. He may not receive other personal satisfactions.

To the materially oriented person, the purpose of the organization or activity is not vitally important. Purposes can be neglected or changed as long as this does not affect his reward. Methods, practices, or procedures may be changed and he will not object if the change does not inconvenience him unduly or affect his rewards.

Example: A man works in a factory in return for wages received. He may have no interest in the product. He may not derive much personal satisfaction from his work. He simply gets paid.

Solidary Incentives

Description: The person receives a reward other than material. Such rewards include enjoyment of the activity, fulfillment of social needs, prestige, power, personal development, approval, satisfying basic drives.

To the solidary type person, the ultimate purpose of the organization is not of major concern. Neglect or even change it, and this person is not likely to object. But change the *way* things are done? Never, unless he clearly sees how the change will enhance the personal rewards he is receiving, for these come from the nature of the activity itself. Change the way things are done, and you may deprive him of his satisfactions.

Example: A woman belongs to the garden club because she enjoys being with the other women. The atmosphere is pleasant. She receives recognition and honor. She fulfills a basic aesthetic interest.

Purposeful Incentives

Description: Material or personal satisfactions are not pri-mary reasons for participating. The person believes in what the organization or activity is striving to accomplish and wants to help.

The purposeful individual is all-out for getting the job done. The purpose must be the target toward which every energy is directed. He becomes dissatisfied if the purpose is neglected or progress toward achieving that purpose is too little or too slow. He is likely to drive himself and his associates. Changing the purpose is out of the question. Procedure is another matter. This person is impatient with procedures that he considers ineffective or irrelevant. If there is anything he cannot tolerate, it is pointlessness. He resents wasting time and resources in any activity that does not help move toward goal achievement.

Example: A parent who has lost a child to cancer devotes himself to the cancer society. He wants to see the disease eradi-cated and is committed to helping achieve this purpose.

Material incentives have less relevance to the church than the others. Christians should operate on a combination of sol-idary and purposeful incentives. We ought to be committed to Christ's purpose and we ought to receive many personal satis-factions in the process. However, some church people are more solidary while others are more purposeful.

The solidary person belongs to the church *primarily* because it satisfies some private personal needs. He is not really com-mitted to the other purposes of the church; therefore, progress in these directions is not a matter of great concern (unless used as a subterfuge for argument or complaint—his behavior will reveal whether his concern is genuine or not). But don't try to change the way things are being done, even though the changes promise to help get the broader purpose accom-plished. He has found his satisfactions in the *way* things are being done. At best, this individual's understanding of purpose is incomplete. At worst, he is a self-seeking person and may, in fact, be in rebellion against the lordship of Christ. It has been typical of men from the time of Eden to want their own way rather than God's way.

The purposeful person wants to see the goal being achieved. He becomes dissatisfied if he cannot see progress. His attitude is: change the way we do things if necessary, but let's get on with the task. He may support activities that seem pointless to him, but he will do so reluctantly out of a sense of duty.

Purposeful and solidary people have difficulty understanding each other. The purposeful person cannot understand why the solidary person is so set in his ways and so unconcerned about the objectives. The solidary person is puzzled by the "fanatic" who is always pushing and trying to upset things. (The material person shakes his head and wonders why those other people are so concerned about things that don't matter anyway.) Much of the unrest and conflict in congregations may be the result of the friction between these two types of orientation toward the church.

Another problem produced by conflicting incentives is that of incomplete membership. Christians live with tensions caused by the presence of both solidary and purposive tendencies within them. We want to fulfill Christ's mission, but we also want to stay as we are. When a person's reason for being a member of the church is not completely the same as the church's reason for existence, his membership is only partial. He will not always strive to achieve the total purpose of the church, and may actually resist the pursuit of that purpose. The strength with which a member supports the goals of the church depends on the compatibility of those goals with his own.

Here, in the private purposes that members hold for the church, is another reason for the decline of churches. Solidary churches typically seek their own satisfaction. Members bend the church to serve their own private preferences. Growth of the church is not seen as an urgent goal and may indeed be seen as undesirable. Many churches simply do not want to grow because private satisfactions have the priority. (It must be remembered, however, that solidary needs are also inherent in the very nature of the church's purpose.)

Congregations tend to become more and more like themselves. That is, a primarily solidary church will not attract or hold purposeful people. These people will gravitate toward a congregation that seems to be on the move and getting the job done. A church that is strongly purposeful will not attract or hold solidary people. These people, too, will gravitate toward their own kind.

The congregation that has a strong mixture of types is likely to be in persistent conflict. A solidary congregation may also be in conflict because people are striving to attain divergent personal satisfactions. A purposeful congregation may also have conflict, but differences among its people tend to occur over the best ways to get the job done.

As a result of the inner ambivalence of Christians and the interaction of members of the church, the operating purpose of the church will be determined by how the balance of power tips to commit the church to certain directions and behaviors.

The operating incentives in churches, as well as other organizations, tend to shift in the direction of the solidary and away from the purposeful. As this happens, the focus moves more toward means than ends, goals are moderated toward the lowest common denominator, and congregations become increasingly inflexible. Leadership is the function that counteracts this trend and builds purposefulness in a body of people.

Means-Ends Commitments

The four possible combinations of attitudes toward means and ends are classified in Figure 9-1. These classifications may describe individuals, congregations, and majorities or minorities in a congregation.

	High Commitment to Ends	Low Commitment to Ends
High Commitment to Means	A	B
Low Commitment to Means	C	D

Figure 9-1. Commitment to means and ends among congregation members.

Type A people are committed to ends or objectives and are convinced their means are effective in achieving those objectives. In such a case, all people have to do is get on with the task. They know where they are going and how to get there. They are strong-minded and may tend to be rigid; but they may also be open to change if persuaded that other means are more productive. These are hard-driving people; and if enough of them are in a congregation, it is likely to be a productive, growing church.

Type D people are not highly committed to the objectives of the church or to means. They are apathetic, indifferent, or alienated. Such an attitude, if it is widespread, is symptomatic of a dying church.

Type B people are more committed to familiar forms, programs, and practices than to high achievement in terms of ultimate purposes. They are satisfied to execute familiar procedures whether or not they are effective. They will resist change, no matter how well it promises to achieve the professed objectives. A congregation of those people will be low in accomplishment and ritualistic.

Type C people are committed to the objectives, but are open and flexible in matters pertaining to means. They would agree with Edison: "There is a better way. Find it!" Enough of these people will produce an innovative, progressive, and ultimately effective congregation.

This typology also suggests a way to classify consensus or disagreement in a congregation regarding objectives and means, as in Figure 9-2:

A Type A congregation is in agreement on objectives and means. Watch them go!

A Type D congregation is fragmented. They do not agree on anything. Watch them go—out of existence.

A Type B congregation is likely to be fairly placid. People may have different objectives in mind, but they agree on the way things are being done. Little progress is likely to be made toward any objective, since the people are probably ritualists and the disagreement over objectives is merely academic.

A Type C congregation has problems, but they are honest problems and likely can be resolved. The important factor is that they agree on what they are trying to achieve. If this congregation will collect enough information, weigh alternatives, and perhaps experiment, it may be even more productive than Type A (which might have agreed on means prematurely and without sufficient research).

	Consensus on Ends	Disagreement on Ends
Consensus on Means	A	B
Disagreement on Means	C	D

Figure 9-2. Consensus on means and ends among congregation members.

Interpersonal Relations

Since interaction among people is required by the basic nature of the church, interpersonal processes can get in the way of the church's pursuit of its authentic purpose. Paul addressed such problems in his letters to churches. People were taking sides against each other for personal reasons not related to the nature, task, or mission of the church.[1] It may be that cultural differences contributed to this party spirit as people rallied to men with whom they could identify. Some Christians were entering into litigation, and leading figures were in conflict.[3] John found himself opposed by Diotrephes who sought to elevate his own status and authority.[4] Such situations deflect attention from the purpose of the church.

People do not automatically drop their psychological and social mechanisms when they become Christians. Inner tensions, ambivalences, aberrations, or hostilities are often projected into Christian interaction. Problem people may be safely assumed to be people with personal problems yet unresolved. The person who continues in unrepented sin may become a bitter critic of others and a focal point of conflict. Unresolved guilt, lack of self-acceptance, or poor self-image also can contaminate church relationships and efforts to function together. Habitual styles of interacting with others can complicate an individual's efforts to function in the life of a congregation.

Work roles affect the way people interact in the church setting. Those in executive positions at work may be able to set goals and develop plans, but unable to carry out the tasks involved. People who follow someone else's orders on the job may be able to carry out details in church projects, but unable to develop goals and plans. The person who is dominated at work or at home may behave like a tyrant in the only place he finds it possible to exert himself.

The complexities of human interaction, if not recognized and managed, can absorb the attention and energies of a congregation to the neglect of its true purpose.

Some fairly safe generalizations may be made about people:

1. They hurt—physically, emotionally, spiritually, or all three.

2. They don't like themselves very well. This includes the boisterous, swaggering braggart. The braggart probably likes himself less than most people do. It is his way of compensating.

3. They tend to solve their problems in self-defeating ways. The insecure man who hides behind the flamboyant, boasting exterior needs appreciation more than anything else to bolster his sagging self-image. But the way he behaves tends to make others try to "put him down," which only makes his problem worse so that he intensifies his irritating behavior. The same vicious circle may be observed in many other problems of human behavior.

4. They need attention, reassurance, acceptance, affirmation, and understanding.

5. They tend to follow the crowd.

6. They are capable of greater accomplishments and more nobility than they usually manifest.

Group Dynamics

In the last several decades, much attention has been given to the way groups of people operate. Each group takes on characteristics of its own, and the group's processes may be quite complex and subtle. These processes strongly affect the way the group relates to its apparent purpose.[5]

Many of the frustrations of working with people could be alleviated by understanding what is really happening and what causes it—in a board meeting, for example. Armed with such an understanding, a leader is much more likely to help develop healthy group action.

When problems arise in a group, people tend to react in one or more of five ways:

1. Fighting. People sometimes express their frustrations in aggression (verbally, non-verbally, and sometimes physically) on each other, or on some other person who happens to be handy. Not all hostile treatment should be taken personally. Defensiveness or counter-hostility, then, is an unwholesome response. (The Bible is loaded with brilliant advice about such matters, if we have the wisdom to follow it.)

2. *Flight.* Some people drop out. Others remain physically present, but withdraw into silence or refusal to participate.

3. *Pairing.* Some people gravitate to others who feel as they do (or can be persuaded to take their side). They support one another in the problem situation.

4. *Dependency.* Other people retreat and seek security by turning to some strong leader-figure. They depend on him to reduce the confusion and solve the problem.

5. *Team problem solving.* In a mature group relationship, people face the problem together. They define and analyze it and set about to solve it.

A group may have a formal goal, yet expend most of its effort on goals that are quite different. It may spend most of its time on tasks that arise out of the solidary needs of the group itself. It may have a stated agenda but really be working on a "hidden agenda," perhaps known only to one or a few, and sometimes hidden from everyone in the group.

A group often develops roles, subgroups or coalitions, informal power centers, norms, communication systems, ways of responding to problems, decision-making habits, rituals, and other procedures that powerfully affect its ability to accomplish its purpose.

These processes can enhance or handicap the degree to which the group's purpose is accomplished. Exciting potential exists in the concept that groups can learn teamwork skills that will intensify their ability to achieve goals.[6] However, unless group processes are understood and ways are found to cope with them constructively, they are often counterproductive to the church's pursuit of its purpose.

For Further Reading

Bormann, Ernest, et. al. *Interpersonal Communication in the Modern Organization.* Riverside, NJ: Free Press, 1961.
Bormann, Ernest G. and Nancy. *Effective Committees and Groups in the Church.* Minneapolis: Augsburg Press, 1973.
Knowles, Malcolm and Hulda. *Introduction to Group Dynamics.* New York: Association Press, 1972.
Leas, Speed and Paul Kittlaus. *Church Fights: Managing Conflicts in the Local Church.* Philadelphia: Westminster Press, 1972.
Richards, Larry. *A New Face for the Church.* Grand Rapids: Zondervan, 1970.

----

[1]This concept was suggested by an unpublished paper, *Incentive Systems: A Theory of Organizations,* by Peter B. Clark and James Q. Wilson. Further information on the theory are provided by: Chester Marnard, *The Functions of the Executive* (Cambridge: Harvard University Press, 1938); Herbert A. Simon, *Administrative Behavior* (New York, 1959); Edward C. Banfield, *Political Influence* (Glencoe, 1961); and James Q. Wilson, *Negro Politics: The Search for Leadership* (Glencoe, 1960).

[2]1 Corinthians 1:10-17; 3:1-4

[3]1 Corinthians 6:1-8; Philippians 4:2

[4]3 John 9, 10

[5]For an introduction to group dynamics with application to the church, see: Ernest G. and Nancy Bormann, *Effective Committees and Groups in the Church* (Minneapolis: Augsburg Publishing Company, 1973).

[6]For an introduction to training for teamwork and participation see: *Participation Training for Adult Education* by Paul Bergevin and John McKinley (St. Louis: Bethany Press, 1965), and *Group Discussion as Learning Process* by Elizabeth Flynn and John LaFaso (New York: Paulist Press, 1972).

Part Four

SOLUTIONS

Section Outline

10. *Leadership and Purpose*
    A. The Christian Style of Leadership
    B. Leaders of the Church
    C. Types of Leaders
    D. Protecting the Leadership Function
    E. Summary

11. *Principles for Leaders*
    A. Personal Growth
    B. Personal Relations
    C. Motivating Others
    D. Summary

12. *Plans and Strategies*
    A. Foundations for Program Planning
    B. Basic Clarification
    C. Diagnosing the Congregation
    D. Diagnosing the Community
    E. Programming

13. *Change Does Not Have to Be a Nightmare*
    A. The Change Process
    B. Guidelines for Change

Conclusion

The effective local congregation clearly understands its nature and purpose, deliberately pursues its mission, and intelligently controls those processes that might weaken or deflect its purpose. Its members are committed to that purpose. They are equipped to pursue it, and they are unified in the venture. Such a congregation carries out its life and work through the power of the Holy Spirit, and it is guided in all this by competent leadership.

The church must have leaders who:
hold God's ideals for it without compromise,
perceive its failures with mature judgment,
believe in it enthusiastically and optimistically,
understand its human weaknesses as well as its divine
strengths, and
can assist it to attain the qualities God intends.

Diagnostic insight, or the ability to determine the nature and cause of a problem, is also basic to leadership in the church. Unfortunately a pattern of diagnosis and flight has developed within the vocational ministry. A minister assumes leadership of a congregation and fulfills his duties until the problems of the situation become apparent. When this point is reached, he begins to assume this ministry is hopeless and to think of moving on. In reality, he is ready only at that moment to begin his ministry with the congregation. Under the diagnosis and flight pattern, however, problems are repeatedly identified but never solved.

This final section discusses the leadership of the church, and ways that leadership can help bring about solutions to the problems that hinder the church's pursuit of God's purpose for it.

CHAPTER

10

Leadership and Purpose

As you read, think about these questions:
—What is leadership? In what way is leadership *the* solution to the problems of churches?
—How do Christian styles and relationships in leadership differ from those commonly observed in the world?
—How can the leadership function in the church best be maintained and protected?

When a disease can be cured simply by administering a particular medication, that medicine is said to be a "specific" for the disease. For example, penicillin is the specific for certain infections. When the infection occurs, penicillin can be administered and the infection is cured.

For many problems in the church, leadership is the specific. Leadership is the function that fosters and maintains a congregation's focus on divine purpose, promotes rational efforts to achieve it, and keeps counterproductive processes in abeyance.

Following a comprehensive study of leadership, a major business corporation stated this definition of a leader: "One who can generate, communicate, and sustain commonality of purpose." Douglas Hyde attributes the success of Communist leaders to "their ability to fire the imagination, create a sense of dedication and send their followers into effective, meaningful action."[1]

Leadership operates between two poles: people on one hand, and their goals on the other. It is the function of helping that body of people move toward achieving their goals. Whoever does this is exerting leadership.

When progress is being made or success achieved, somebody is causing it. Inertia can just happen, but movement is caused. When a church is alive, effective, and progressing, somebody is emphasizing, clarifying, and reminding people of their purpose; somebody is keeping objectives in the spotlight; somebody is showing people how to merge their efforts to accomplish their common goals; somebody is challenging and inspiring others. In other words, somebody is leading. *Leadership is the key to effective congregations.*

The Christian Style of Leadership

Jesus sharply contrasts two approaches to leadership—one that is appropriate to Christian relationships and one that is not:

> You know that the rulers of the Gentiles lord it over them, and their high officials exercise authority over them. Not so with you. Instead, whoever wants to become great among you must be your servant, and whoever wants to be first must be your slave—just as the Son of Man did not come to be served, but to serve, and to give his life as a ransom for many.[2]

The authoritarian relationship between leader and follower is the one common to the world. From a position above the people, such leaders exercise authority down upon those under them. The typical organizational chart of such institutions is pyramidal; it traces a downward branching of an authority system. Jesus' teaching was called forth because two of His disciples assumed His kingdom would have such an authority system and wanted chief offices. They had failed to understand the character of His kingdom and the nature of its leadership.

Jesus sets forth a relationship between leader and people in which servant-leadership is to prevail. The leader in this case is not *over* but *among* people. The role is not one of authority but of service. The leader serves the ones who are led by helping them make progress; in relationship, he is their slave. Jesus discards once and for all the secular ruler model for His people and replaces it with a relationship that He himself first exemplified. Such a leader is a facilitator-enabler-equipper; his role is that of helping the body of people become functional in achieving their purposes.

The leader functions best as a trusted friend. We do not commit ourselves to our critics or judges but to affirmers who understand us, accept us, and help us develop. People followed Jesus because He came not to condemn, but to open the gates to new life.

The group responds best to a leader who is perceived as "one of us." Acceptance must flow both ways between leader and group. An open, cooperative, sympathetic relationship is the best climate in which leadership functions.

The prime means for leadership are the Word of God and personal example. Thus, preaching and teaching are focal points for the exercise of leadership. The right to lead comes from such personal qualities as clarity of vision, the ability to facilitate progress toward the goal, personal integrity, and competence in equipping people through the Word.

The servant-leader helps the body of people perceive their goals, develop commitment to them, mobilize to reach them, and pursue their achievement. He offers guidance, inspiration, instruction, and resources; but he strives to work in cooperation with the group as a team.

Authority and authoritarianism should not be confused. Authoritarianism says, "This is right because I say so." Authority says, "I say this because it is right." A good leader has authority on his side but he is not authoritarian.

The ability to move people arises out of a persuasion-consensus process rather than an arbitrary order-obedience one. Nothing creates better cooperation than a leader who does his homework, keeps abreast of developments, keeps on top of details, and has established a good track record for being right. A good leader does not tell people he is an authority. If he is an authority, he does not need to; if he isn't, they will know it.

The authoritarian leader seeks to be in full command, directing every detail of the church. Followers are supposed to function simply by carrying out his plans and orders. Such a leader sometimes gets fast, if temporary, results. Over the long view, however, his followers tend to become passive. Their competence declines and their motivation becomes difficult to maintain. The empire-builder frequently ends up without an empire. Over the long term, the authoritarian—whether in the pulpit, on the board, or in the pew—seldom really helps the kingdom achieve its purpose as effectively as the servant-leader. The pyramidal authority system is one of control rather than of facilitation, and often creates a static condition rather than a goal-effective one.

In some ways it is easier to be an authoritarian than a servant-leader. The latter requires more skill, greater discipline of attitude and behavior, and a clearer understanding of the task than does the former. But the rewards are far greater.

> Now the Gentile idea of greatness is inverted, turned upside down, the pyramid resting on its apex, the great man not sitting atop lesser men, but the great man bearing the lesser men on his back.[3]

The highest emblem of Christian leadership is not the whip of the lion tamer, but the towel and basin. The lion tamer stance is not nearly as effective in dealing with people as is the humble servant. The great leader must portray the Christ who sacrifices His all for His people, and in the process awakens inward music and inflames hearts to carry out ideals, to achieve divine goals.

Leaders of the Church

Christian leaders help congregations discover who they are, why they are here, where they ought to be, where they are now, what resources and opportunities they have, what problems and needs exist, and how to get from where they are to where they ought to be.

Leaders help individual efforts add up to something. They help the entire congregation develop a framework of shared commitments to the task and to the means for accomplishing it. They act as catalysts, helping individuals to meld their abilities together as the body of Christ. They keep organizational processes and cultural expectations from getting in the way of accomplishing the task. They help Christians strengthen their purposefulness through a growing commitment to Christ and His kingdom. They help individuals and the congregation to be aware of the progress they are making toward their goals.

Leadership in the church was once thought of in terms of

holding an office or having a certain title or position. It was equated with authority, viewed as a matter of directing or controlling other people, and thought to reside in specific people.

A more dynamic view of leadership is emerging. According to this view, leadership is a function rather than a position. As such it can and should be shared by all members of a group as they have opportunity. Leadership, then, is not identical with office-holding. It is not the exclusive right of designated persons, but a function that should be provided by any Christian who has the opportunity. The apostle Paul made it clear that achieving the purpose of the church is the business of all Christians.[4] His description of the church as the body of Christ also emphasizes this fact.[5] The whole congregation is to be an effective team. Any Christian is leading when he helps the team remember its purpose and generate positive action to move toward the goal.

This view of leadership in no way denies the importance of designated leaders who may be thought of as coordinators, enablers, or equippers of the team. The leadership of the church should be a core group of people who are especially competent in Biblical knowledge, spiritual qualities, maturity, and leadership skills. This group may center in one or more specially trained and salaried persons. Many functions may be generally shared by a congregation and yet be focused in certain individuals. For example, service (or ministry) should be shared by all Christians, but it is especially centered in deacons (servants). The same is true with evangelism and evangelists, teaching and teachers, shepherding (caring for persons) and pastors or elders. These functions, as well as preaching and general administrative ministry, may center in salaried persons with particular abilities or training, who devote undivided attention to their specialized functions.

Leadership Roles

Two major functions of leadership are those of *expressive* and *instrumental* operations.

Expressive operations are those that create and maintain in a body of people a vital commitment to a clear and shared purpose. These operations point the way, guide, motivate, challenge, inspire, devise and execute plans, instruct, enable people to function well, and keep the vision clear. They center on stating, re-stating, reminding, and clarifying purpose. They interpret actions and efforts in terms of how they contribute to achieving the purpose. They serve as the "eyes" for the body to see where it is and where it is going.

The major functions of expressive servant-leaders include: (1) exhorting, encouraging, or urging people toward the goal; and (2) correcting, reproving, rebuking, and exhorting people back on the track to the goal when they have deflected.[6] Expressive concerns focus in the general oversight tasks and communication functions such as preaching and teaching.

Instrumental operations deal with finding and marshalling resources, developing ways and means, and administering programs for achieving the purpose.

In a local congregation, the Biblical roles of elder and deacon naturally follow the expressive-instrumental functions of leadership. Elders, also referred to as pastors and bishops or overseers, give general oversight to the congregation and the persons who constitute it. Their main functions are those of guarding the identity and direction of the congregation, clarifying and emphasizing purpose, establishing policy and goals, keeping the counterproductive processes from undermining the dynamic of the congregation, developing strategies for implementing the mission of the church in its given time and place, and constantly generating momentum for goal achievement. They must be spiritual pacesetters and guides.

Deacons are most appropriately instrumental leaders who take the general intentions of the elders and ministers, carry out the details of planning, and administer the various functions so that desired ends are accomplished in the life and work of the congregation.

Preaching ministers are also expressive leaders. They are at the center of the leadership core, at the hub of the communications network within the congregation, and the major contact with the broader church world. They also have the advantage of special training, and their time is usually devoted to the church in a unique way since the congregation provides for their livelihood. Their major task must be the communicating of God's intentions to the congregation. These leaders, then, must devote themselves primarily to such functions as study of the Bible; preparation, preaching, and teaching; prayer, helping the congregation establish directions; training other Christians to function effectively in the congregation and in the world as Christ's agents. It is imperative that preaching ministers be as free as possible from instrumental details in order to concentrate on purposes, objectives, goals, and ideals.

If a congregation salaries other staff members, these persons may share the expressive function, concentrate on instrumental concerns, or, most likely, combine the two functions. In some congregations staff ministers function as the primary expressive leaders in specialized aspects of the church's life and work. They may be designated as youth ministers, Christian education ministers, ministers of music, and the like. They, in turn, function with a number of volunteers fulfilling instrumental roles. For example, the youth minister may give general oversight and planning to his area of specialization in concert with the elders and other staff members. Subsequently, he recruits and trains sponsors who implement the details of the ministry with youth as instrumental leaders.

Types of Leaders

As with other functions, leadership may occur in the positive, neutral, or negative modes. If the church has positive leaders, then it may also have neutrals who neither help nor hinder. There may also be persons who muddy the focus on purpose and goals, hinder their fulfillment, and disrupt the team. These persons might be considered "anti-leaders."

Anti-leaders may be vague or confused about the nature and purpose of the church. They may be more concerned about forms, practices, or their own pet concerns than about getting the real task of the church done. They may be more oriented toward means, forms, traditions, or institutional concerns than toward objectives. They may have private incentives for which they are seeking satisfaction. They may be absorbed by a cultural version of the church. They may be inept in the areas of interpersonal relationships or teamwork. In short, they are part of the problem rather than part of the solution.

If leadership is a function, it may also be said that not everyone who is appointed or elected to office actually exercises leadership. Leadership is not automatically vested by an act of installation.

Official leaders should be chosen from those who have demonstrated informal positive leadership. The ideal process does not make a Christian a leader by giving him an office; it recognizes leadership and makes such people officials. This kind of

Leadership Function

	Positive	Neutral	Negative
Official	1	2	3
Non-official	4	5	6

Figure 10-1. Six possible postures of leadership in the local church.

leadership is self-authenticating as it rises to the surface. Leadership is first earned and granted, then it is made official. Paul's discussion of elders and deacons provides the identifying marks by which leaders can be recognized and selected for these offices.[7]

The relationship between office-holding and the positive, neutral, and negative exercise of leadership function is visualized in Figure 10-1. Six types of persons are identified in the diagram.

Type 1 holds an office and is exerting positive leadership. The congregation is blessed if it has a corps of these people. This is the Biblical ideal for a congregation.[8]

Type 2 holds an office but is not leading. Neither is he a disrupter. His own inertia is transmitted to the congregation. The New Testament knows nothing of non-functioning or static officers. The only real leaders are those who function as active goal-seekers, helping the body of people move toward their objectives. Leadership is by definition dynamic.

Type 3 holds an office, but he is a disrupter or hinderer of the progress of the church. It is a disaster for a congregation to have many such people. The Bible also speaks of this problem.[9]

Type 4 does not hold an office, but he helps lead the congregation. People who have studied leadership and group processes have properly pointed out the difference between formal and informal structures in organizations. The formal structure identifies those persons who nominally occupy various positions or offices. In terms of function, however, it may be that persons who have never been officially assigned to do so are the ones who actually fulfill the functions of those positions. This is the informal or operational structure. In most cases the formal and informal structures will overlap, but seldom are they identical; and so a distinction may be drawn between formal and informal leaders.

Type 5 does not hold office and does not help lead. He is a spectator. The church should not resemble a football game with a handful of men down on the field desperately needing rest, being watched by ten thousand spectators desperately needing exercise. The church should be more like an army in which every person is responsibly involved. In an army, everyone is committed to helping win the war, not just the designated officers. Whenever the humblest private is helping spur the troops to victory, he is *functioning* as a leader, even without the rank.

Type 6 is not an office holder and he disrupts and hinders the progress of the church. This person often sees himself as an important client of the church. The church—its minister and its program—ought to satisfy his private wishes, meet his expectations, or serve him, whether or not this fits the Biblical ideal of the church and its purpose. This person is often a troubled individual. His church behavior is simply a symptom of his personal inadequacies or dysfunctions.

A word of clarification is in order regarding Types 3 and 6. Simply because he opposes ideas or decisions does not necessarily imply a person is a negative influence. Opposing error is positive. It is productive of Christ's purpose. Paul was functioning in a positive mode in opposing certain errors.[10] However, a wise maxim says, "If you kick be sure you kick toward the goal." Christians must be careful that when they oppose certain things, they are making a positive contribution to the right goal and not simply expressing a counterproductive reaction.

Protecting the Leadership Function

As with purpose and objectives in the church, the leadership function is vulnerable to erosion and must be protected. Leadership can best be protected by maintaining a balance between the kinds of leadership responsibility.

Maintenance and Task Accomplishment

Maintenance keeps the organization healthy; task orientation keeps it moving. Both concerns are legitimate and necessary. The problem is one of keeping a proper balance of these concerns so that one does not overpower the other. Figure 10-2 illustrates such a balance between these two concerns.

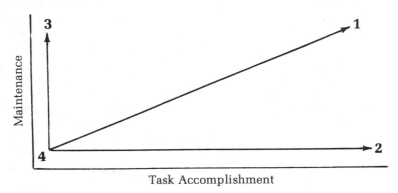

Figure 10-2. Roles of maintenance and task accomplishment in the work of a church leader.

The best possible leader (1) achieves a balance between maintenance and task. He devotes enough attention to maintenance to keep the organization in good working order. He is sensitive to persons and their needs and to interpersonal relationships. But he also devotes enough attention to task requirements to accomplish the purpose of the organization. He gives attention both to mission and to harmony. Jesus demonstrated a perfect balance in this regard. He could correct people when necessary but comfort them when that was needed. He challenged people but was also profoundly considerate of them. At times he prodded them and at times he tenderly and humbly served them. He could issue ringing commissions and wash His people's feet.

The hard-driving goal achiever (2) may leave people bleeding in a cloud of dust. He gives little attention to the people with whom he works—their welfare, happiness, satisfaction, or interpersonal relations—he is intent only on getting the job done.

Organizational health is only a side issue and given little concern in relation to the task. In the long run, however, he accomplishes less than the ideal leader, because the organization becomes diseased and the task eventually suffers. In his insensitivity to his people he digs traps that will eventually cause his downfall. Since good relationships among Christians in the body of Christ are themselves part of the Lord's objective, maintenance and task are even more closely related than in other instances. Accomplishing some goals at the expense of intended relationships is a distortion in the church that will eventually cause the downfall of such a leader.

The static relationship builder (3) is excessively concerned about keeping everybody happy. He will do almost anything to keep peace and harmony. He is overly sensitive about his relationships with other people, and not very effective about getting the job done. The ironic fact is, maintenance eventually crumbles because morale and other health factors of the organization suffer from of lack of accomplishment. Both he and the hard-driving goal achiever are self-defeating.

Finally, there is the bureaucrat (4). He has one concern: following the rules and procedures and preserving his own position. Both maintenance and task languish. He simply follows the routines. The bureaucrat, too, must be ultimately self-defeating, for self-preservation succeeds only as long as the system can be maintained.

Both maintenance and task functions, then, must be kept in balance if leadership is to be protected and the church may be purposeful and productive.

Expressive and Instrumental Operations

If expressive functions serve as the eyes of the body, to clarify goals and guide people toward them, instrumental ones would be the nerves and muscles to implement goal achievement. Expressive functions deal with "why;" instrumental ones with "how."

Expressive and instrumental operations are equally necessary, and complement one another to enable the body of people to succeed in their task. Expressive activity that is not implemented by operation is visionary. Instrumental activity that is not channeled by expressive direction is chaotic.

An ever-present tendency is for instrumental concerns to dominate or even supplant expressive ones. "How" tends to overshadow and dictate to the "Why." This weakens the role of purpose, and we are back to the problem of means-ends reversal or displacement. In one highly achieving congregation, questions of ways, means, and costs are never discussed in the planning process until the idea in question is thoroughly considered in terms of how necessary it is to the progress of Christ's work. In other congregations such instrumental considerations abort many promising opportunities.

In churches, the problem of dominant instrumental concerns can be seen in preoccupation with operational details to the neglect of expressive functions. It occurs in board meetings, congregational meetings, committee meetings, and in the daily activities of ministers. Ministers, elders, and other expressive officers tend to become weighed down with instrumental details. When this occurs, vision dims and people lose sight of purpose.

The apostles, with their divine guidance, were among the few expressive leaders in history who avoided the trap of instrumental enslavement. When instrumental imperatives (fair and impartial benevolence for the widows) threatened to deflect their primary functions in the early church, the apostles stood firm in protecting their roles. They insisted that this concern be delegated to others.[11] They did not deny the necessity of the instrumental function, but they prevented it from dominating the higher-priority expressive function of prayer and the ministry of the Word. Neither did they minimize the value of the instrumental function as somehow beneath them. This function is not for "second rate" people or for those who have not yet arrived at levels deserving of higher honor. Note the high qualities the apostles instructed the church to look for in the men to be appointed to these tasks. The apostles were not "too good" to do these tasks. They simply recognized the need for division of labor and the protecting of their necessary role.

Expressive and instrumental operations must be in proper balance, with expressive functions coming ahead of instrumental ones, providing meaning and direction. Some persons should specialize in expressive concerns, others in instrumental operations. If these are not generally separated, persons who should be providing expressive leadership tend to become embroiled in ways and means, to the dimming of vision. This arrangement is wisely provided for in the church through the dual offices of elders (expressive leaders) and deacons (instrumental leaders). The key to this arrangement, however, is that persons in these positions must function; they must actually exert leadership. Technical replication of this pattern without the positive exercise of functional leadership does not produce a church that accomplishes God's purpose.

Symptoms Indicating Lack of Effective Leadership

When congregational problems are discussed, the most common difficulties cited do not usually revolve around deep doctrinal or philosophical concerns. The problems most frequently lamented include the following:

1. Poor interpersonal relationships among members or between members and those in offices. Inability of people to understand each other, friction, conflict, criticism, and general lack of ability to get along with each other—to say nothing of working together productively.

2. Aimlessness or inertia. Inability of people to rally to a common direction or purpose.

3. Puzzling attitudes and behaviors among the members. Unjustified demands or expectations for the church or minister. Inadequate views of their own roles as Christians in the congregation.

4. Ineffective programs, irrational policies, pointless routines, or useless traditions that defy efforts to change them.

5. Low morale, lack of motivation, indifference, irresponsibility, pessimism, and poor cooperation (indicated by low attendance, inadequate finances, lack of workers).

6. Preoccupation with trivial details to the neglect of primary responsibilities of the church.

All those problems are symptoms of failure in the role of purpose. This in turn reflects a need for leaders who understand the nature of the church, the principles of working with people, and the principles of effective leadership.

Summary

In vigorous, effective congregations, the following conditions prevail:

1. The entire body of people is committed to achieving a clear, authentic, dominant purpose.

2. They act in a deliberate and rational way to accomplish that purpose.

3. They prevent hindrances from obscuring or displacing that purpose.

4. Their leadership helps them to function in this way.

5. Leadership is vigorously and wisely exerted.

6. Leadership is widely distributed throughout the body on an informal basis.

7. Officers have first proved themselves leaders and are then placed in office.

8. Officers do not simply hold positions; they actively exercise leadership as a function.

9. The expressive aspect of leadership is protected and gives direction to instrumental leadership. Some persons specialize in expressive functions; others, in instrumental functions.

10. Leadership is of the Christian servant-leader type rather than of the authoritarian type.

11. Leadership gives concerned care to the well-being of the body of people and to goal achievement, and is therefore dynamic rather than static.

12. The pulpit and classroom are focal points for expressive leadership.

13. Leadership builds the broadest possible base of responsible and competent participation in the congregation in which people share: dreaming for the future, setting goals, developing and carrying out plans, shouldering responsibility for achievement or failure, mustering resources, and evaluating progress.

14. Leadership vigorously pursues both edification and increase of the body through evangelism. The commitment to both kinds of growth is unquenchable.

Leadership is the function of helping people: (1) to realize their common purpose and keep their attention focused on it; (2) to think clearly, act intelligently, and muster resources to achieve their purpose; (3) to work together as a team.

The leader, in order to function effectively, must follow certain guidelines. He guards his own purposefulness and rationality. He is future-oriented, in contrast to plodders who live for the moment, and retreaters who live in the past. He has overarching objectives and does not spend so much time engrossed in the problems or details of the moment that he loses the long view. He does not wait for circumstances to arise and then *react*; he *acts* in the direction of Christ's goals.

He models and demonstrates Christian commitment. He is out in front of the people, leading—not pushing. He is constantly communicating purpose and meaning, sharing with the congregation his own strong positive expectations, investing every activity and event with meaning, generating goal-oriented thinking in the people.

Given such conditions, the church is enabled to grow and build itself up in love as each part does its work.[12]

For Further Reading

Anderson, James. *To Come Alive!* New York: Harper and Row, 1973.

Engstrom, Ted and Edward Dayton. *The Art of Management for Christian Leaders.* Waco, TX: Word Books, 1976.

Getz, Gene. *Sharpening the Focus of the Church.* Chicago: Moody Press, 1974.

Hyde, Douglas. *Dedication and Leadership.* Notre Dame, IN: University of Notre Dame, 1966.

Kilinski, Kenneth and Jerry Wofford. *Organization and Leadership for the Local Church.* Grand Rapids: Zondervan, 1973.

Lindgren, Alvin and Norman Shawchuck. *Management for Your Church.* Nashville: Abingdon, 1977.

Richards, Larry. *A New Face for the Church.* Grand Rapids: Zondervan, 1970.

Schuller, Robert. *Your Church Has Real Possibilities.* Glendale: Regal, 1974.

Wagner, C. Peter. *Your Church Can Grow.* Glendale: Regal, 1976.

---

[1] Douglas Hyde, *Dedication and Leadership* (Notre Dame, IN: University of Notre Dame Press, 1966), p. 12.

[2] Matthew 20:25-28

[3] R.C.H. Lenski, *The Interpretation of St. Matthew's Gospel* (Minneapolis: Augsburg Publishing House, 1943), p. 791.

[4] Ephesians 4:11-16

[5] 1 Corinthians 12:12-27; Romans 12:4-8

[6] 2 Timothy 4:2; Acts 20:17-32

[7] 1 Timothy 3:1-12; Titus 1:6-9

[8] 1 Timothy 3:1-16; 1 Peter 5:1-11; Titus 1:6-11; Ephesians 4:11-16

[9] Acts 20:29, 30; 2 Timothy 2:14-18, 23-26; 4:14, 15; Philippians 1:15, 16; 3 John 9-11

[10] See, for example, Galatians 2:11.

[11] Acts 6:1-7

[12] Ephesians 4:16

Principles
for Leaders

As you read, think about these questions:
—In what ways do a leader's self-improvements tend to enhance his leadership ability?
—What are some characteristics of successful people?
—How can a leader keep involvement and objectivity in balance?
—What are some of the ways a leader can motivate his people?

Since good leadership is so important to healthy, productive congregations, since it is an area of frequent problems, and since it can be learned—what are some principles for improving leadership?

Foundation principle: Effectiveness as a leader depends not only on *what* you do but *how* you go about it. Some people do the right things (theoretically) but they destroy their own effectiveness by their attitudes, the way they relate to other people, and the strategy they use.

Personal Growth

Did you ever try to push a string? It can't be done. The only way you can move it along is to pull from the front. You cannot lead people until you are ahead of them. You cannot lead where you have not gone. You lead best by example.

Become a model of the characteristics or actions you want others to adopt. Be what you want others to be—and more. Do what you want others to do—and more. Team members have the right to say to their leaders, "Don't just tell us. Show us." Not much can happen through us until it has first happened to us. We communicate best that which we are discovering at a personal level.

As a leader, you must keep your own sights clear if you are to help others to do the same. Keep the big picture in view amid the swirl of details. See every move you make in the total perspective of the overall objective. Do not be vague or confused about what you are trying to accomplish, or allow impulsiveness to make you work at cross purposes with yourself. Immerse yourself in the Bible, absorbing the "feel" of it as well as the words. Through prayer build your relationship with God and line up your perspectives with His.

You must be completely sold on what you are doing. In every moment of confusion or disillusionment, your compass must be the conviction that your commissioned purpose and objectives were established by Christ, that they are right, and that they are the most important values in the world.

Keep Growing

Enthusiastically seek to understand the Lord's will more adequately. Seek challenging ideas, helpful insights, and effective methods. According to one researcher, the major difference between successful people and failures is: the successful are always looking for fresh ideas and better ways while the failures do not.

Seek improvement, excellence, and mastery in the area of your leadership. Read widely, talk with others in the field, keep on learning, never complete your education, scour the world for knowledge, wisdom, insights, and resources.

Share with your people the sparkling best of what you are learning. Exciting ideas are a precious commodity for a leader. One outstanding preacher always keeps a book at hand and reads whenever he has a free moment. In an extremely busy ministry this man finds enough of these odd moments to read an average of a book a day. A systematic reading and study program could greatly enhance the effectiveness of most leaders. Churches would be far ahead to help their leaders purchase books and underwrite their participation in various enrichment programs.

Learn to envision a variety of ways to achieve your objectives; do not become locked into one viewpoint. Practice "getting outside" the situation to look at it from different viewpoints and try on various possibilities in your imagination. Clarify the situation by asking the right questions. Think reflectively, ranging about creatively in search of other approaches, avenues, or channels of operation. Creative people are able to view familiar situations through fresh eyes and to find a variety of models through which to analyze the situation. Jesus used parables in a masterful way to accomplish this.

Organize Yourself

Successful people fascinate researchers. One research project identified four characteristics of successful people:

1. They know what they want.
2. They know when they want it.
3. They know how to get it.
4. They discipline themselves. In the lives of these people, every action of every day is calculated to move toward the goal.

Many people scatter their efforts because they do not have a single focus for their lives. Others are unwilling to apply the discipline required to organize their time and efforts to achieve what they want.

Disciplined people achieve some startling accomplishments. Alexander Maclaren wrote his famous and monumental work, *Exposition of the Scripture*, by dedicating to the project just one-half hour before breakfast every day. But it was *every day* for years.

Over a period of forty years, John Wesley traveled on horseback two hundred fifty thousand miles to preach and lead an era of revival. He traveled an average of twenty miles a day, preached 40,000 sermons, wrote 400 books, and learned ten languages. He was distressed that he could not write more than fifteen hours a day—because his eyes were failing at the age of eighty-three. He was chagrined he could not preach more than an average of twice a day—at age eighty-six. His diary records how he deplored an increasing tendency to lie in bed until 5:30 in the morning.

One man of unusual accomplishment listed his own principles for organizing his life:
1. Plan long range.
2. Break long-range plans down into smaller goals.
3. Schedule the short-range goals.
4. Schedule each day's time.
5. Follow the daily schedule.
6. Make maximum use of your time by
   —Listing each day's activities,
   —Assigning priorities to the activities,
   —Delegating as many activities as possible,
   —Scheduling each activity according to priority,
   —Departing from the plan only when absolutely necessary.

One warning about establishing plans and priorities: Leaders and congregations sometimes discuss action, study the situation, and make plans *ad infinitum;* but they never get started doing anything.

It is difficult to muster courage to commit oneself to a course of action. Contemplation is safe. But taking action opens the way for many risks. A good leader helps people get off dead center and start moving at the right time.

> There is no more miserable human being than one in whom nothing is habitual but indecision.
>
> —William James

Good leaders are *future oriented.* Know your overarching objectives. Have goals for today, tomorrow, five years from now, and ten years from now. Do not spend so much time putting out the fires of the moment's problems and details that you lose the long view. Do not wait for circumstances to arise and then *react. Act* in the direction of your goals.

Understand Yourself

Effective leaders are aware of how they affect other people, how other people affect them, and why.

Strive to become aware of your own needs and motivations. To the extent you do this, you are in control; to the extent you fail, you are controlled. Be careful not to use your role as the outlet for your own personality problems, and thereby transmit them to an entire congregation. "Know thyself," is a basic maxim for every leader. Take stock of your mental images. Inventory your thoughts and attitudes. Remember, you are the same size as your ideas.

Pace your efforts. Work with natural cycles, pushing when the time is right and easing up when necessary. If you know where you are going, you can use the particular moment more intelligently, and you can be patient with momentary discouragements. Think big, but temper your dreams with realism.

Personal Relations

Some people draw cooperation from their associates, while others make their associates want to find opportunity to oppose them. The more effective agent of change within the church will operate more as a reformer than as a revolutionary:

Revolutionary	*Reformer*
An outsider, psychologically	An insider
Pushes and forces	Facilitates
Highly visible	Low visibility
Incites	Inspires
Manipulates	Leads
Ethics are situational	Ethics are trustworthy
Egocentric	Exocentric

The person who generates confidence is genuinely concerned about other people, accepts others and their viewpoints, and radiates personal warmth. This person affirms the value of others, maintains a psychological arm-around-the-shoulder stance, and earns the right to be trusted. His relationship with others is not mechanical or manipulative, but is one of mutual respect.

Watch What You Telegraph
You are constantly telegraphing messages to other people by statement, innuendo, posture, facial expression, gesture—by your whole presence. Nonverbal communications are, in some ways, stronger than what is actually said. You may or may not be telegraphing what you intend.

Communication includes an echo. What we communicate bounces back, reflecting what we have beamed out. Frequently we get back just what we deserve; in this area of life the principle of reaping what we sow is especially operative.

In all you communicate—verbally, nonverbally, in print; when you take the initiative and when you respond—ask yourself, "What will people become if this communication is taken seriously?" It can be frightening to imagine what congregations might become when fed the steady diet of some leaders' attitudes as expressed in conversation, from the pulpit, in the classroom, and through the church papers.

Be alert and careful that the message they receive is the same as the one you thought you sent.

Keep Involvement and Objectivity In Balance

Ministers can be wise in allowing their people to know that they, too, are human beings—that they hurt, yearn, fear, and fail, just as the rest of the people do.

A physician was growing concerned about the barriers that existed between him and his patients. He began to realize that they saw him as always well, always a winner, and always right, while they were always sick, losers, and wrong. When he began to share something of his life—good and bad—with them, they began to relate as equals, free to reveal themselves and communicate with him.

A group of church leaders were commiserating with each other about some of their problem people. One member of the group listened silently for a while and then quietly said, "You remind me of a bunch of doctors talking about their patients. What if one said, 'I'm working with a man who has leukemia. I don't know what I'm going to do about him. I just can't stand people with leukemia!' And another said, 'You think that's bad, I have a whole practice made up of people with heart trouble. You've never known what exasperation is until you have to put up with cardiac cases.'

"You're talking about people with problems. Instead of getting so uptight about these people, why not try to understand their 'diseases' and see what can be done to help them get better?"

Churches are made up of people. Not bad people in most cases—just people, people with problems, like all of us. Jesus did not see people as disgusting, but as sick people who needed a physician, and He was willing to serve them in that role.

Leaders need to feel personally identified with the activity of the group. But unless they are also objective, they begin to take personally every problem, criticism, error, or failure. Or they may begin to perceive all progress as personal success. Human beings tend to become defensive about activities with which they are connected. When negative reaction, hostility, or criticism arises, we want to defend ourselves rather than consider the validity of the criticisms or search for solutions.

Most people prefer all negative reactions to be kept below the surface. If they can be brushed aside as insignificant, perhaps others will not notice them. "If these unwelcome intruders can be kept out of sight and ignored, perhaps they will go away," we tend to think.

Effective leaders use dissatisfaction creatively as a means of helping accomplish the objectives. Problems are a signal that confusion or ambiguity exists and ought to be resolved. Something is amiss either in the purposes and programs, or in the relationships among the people. Find the problem and search for solutions. Don't damage your own effectiveness by becoming defensive. Don't try to squelch the symptoms; look for and solve the problems to which they point.

Empathize with people. Put yourself in their place. See things as through their eyes. Deal with them from *their* point of view rather than from your own, if you would lead effectively.

Involve as Many People as Possible

Develop a climate of participation so that the maximum number of people share in planning, carrying out, and evaluating efforts to accomplish their purposes.

Don't try to do everything yourself, even when it may seem easier to do so. It is better to involve the people and to keep responsibility at the most individual level possible. Seek to develop leadership in others, to multiply the function and expand it as far as possible.

Cliches about "all leaders and no followers" are based on a false viewpoint that pictures leadership as giving orders and directing others. When leadership is seen as helping move the group toward its objectives, it is a function to be widely shared.

It is your function as leader-equipper to bring the various efforts of many people into an orderly arrangement. Such coordination allows efforts to complement each other rather than work at cross purposes. In this way, movement toward a common objective is smoothly accelerated.

Help people become aware of good teamwork and healthy group process so that they develop their skills of cooperating. (Cooperation is a skill that can be learned.) Share with them as much of the leadership as possible. Let programs be theirs to the maximum extent possible. We support most fully that which we understand and have had a share in discovering or deciding.

Jesus invested much of His work in developing a nucleus of leaders. These leaders, in turn, followed the same procedures, and the leadership (and membership) of the early church multiplied quickly.

What's better than being a leader? Developing others into leaders.

Have Patience

An effective leader knows the value of timing. He will not try to do in a day (or a month) what may take a year. Ideas must be repeated often and over a period of time before their effects can be seen. If a minister fails to realize this fact, he may label a congregation as hopeless if it does not "tune in" to his ideas in a month or a year. He begins to look for a greener pasture — which will probably seem just as hopeless in a few months. What the minister may fail to realize is: 1) He arrived at his level of thinking over a long period of time, but his idea may be entirely new to the congregation. 2) Because of communication filters, they may not even understand what he is saying. 3) It will take time for their points of view to meld together.

Don't run away and leave people behind. Remember, nearly every idea is first rejected, and then accepted only after a lengthy period of time. For this reason the average ministry is probably far too short.

On the office wall of a prominent businessman of a few years ago a motto read: "Don't quit too soon. You may be only three feet away." As a gold prospector he had become thoroughly discouraged, sold his claim, and returned East to go into business. One of the biggest strikes in history was made just three feet from where he had given up. The experience provided his motto for life, and enabled him to become an outstanding success in another vocation.

Significant projects take time. They must be thought through to maturity and planned meticulously. They must be shared with the people who must support and carry them through over a long enough time and thoroughly enough for consensus to build.

Motivating Others

The "gray people" who fill the pews of the churches are the tremendous untapped resources for Christ's cause. These are the overlooked people; they are not in trouble, nor do they exhibit flashy talents, and so they are forgotten. Christians have often been made to feel guilty for their lack of activity but have been provided neither the preparation nor the opportunities to function.

A leader helps and motivates such people to develop their talents and invest them in a worthwhile task. This requires knowledge of the people; sensitivity to their special personalities, feelings, and needs; and willingness to give them the encouragement and support to help them venture into action. The leader provides them opportunities to take action, advises them, helps them solve their problems, and provides the personal acceptance to infuse them with courage.

Hold Proper Expectations

The simplest way to activate a particular behavior in other people is to expect them to act in that way.

Two ministers were discussing their neighborhood. The first remarked how cold and unresponsive people were. He had attempted to make a religious survey in the area and was refused cooperation everywhere. The other minister said he, too, had made a survey and had made over 600 calls without once being refused cooperation. He explained that he had gone into the area expecting people to be cooperative, and they were. When an occasional person seemed about to refuse, he would say, "Oh come now, this is the 410th house I've visited and no one has refused me yet. You aren't going to be the first, are you?" (At number 617, he confessed, the woman simply said "Yes" and closed the door!)

The difference in response was largely created by the attitudes of the ministers involved.

Church leaders often violate these principles and then wonder why people are not motivated to serve. They assume people are more likely to accept appointments if they emphasize that the task requires little time or effort. Such an appeal to mediocrity gives the impression that the task is unimportant. Naturally, people are not movitated. Unimportant activities do not stir men's souls.

Effective leaders have strong positive expectations, which they constantly share among the membership. They avoid cynicism. They expect the best from people, and they usually get it.

Build Confidence

Lack of courage is one of the great paralyzers of human activity. People tend to underestimate their abilities and to underrate their performance. Encouragement, recognition of effort and achievement, and honest praise for success are legitimate ways to motivate Christian effort. Positive thinking is powerful; and emphasis on success builds confidence and positive expectations.

When faced with an opportunity to act, people often are unable to see immediately how the task can be accomplished. The "how" specter frightens them off at the very beginning. The leader can motivate by:

1. Helping define the task.
2. Helping analyze the task to see how it can be done and what it will require.
3. Helping set precise goals.
4. Helping find information or other resources.
5. Offering assistance to complete the task.
6. Helping to review progress periodically. If progress is lacking he helps identify the problem rather than placing blame. If progress is satisfactory, he encourages continued efforts.
7. Providing rewards (at least appreciation) for success.

Human beings have both a need to achieve and a need to avoid failure. The way these needs balance out helps determine whether the person will attempt a given activity. This idea can be expressed in the following equation:

$$NA/NAF = effort$$

If the need to achieve (NA) is stronger than the need to avoid failure (NAF), a person is likely to undertake positive action. But if the need to avoid failure is too strong, the individual probably will shrink back in fear.

An effective leader can strengthen the need to achieve and reduce the fear of failure through acceptance and encouragement. Motivation to action, then, becomes stronger.

When people are indecisive, have difficulty coming to agreement, or persist in pursuing tangents, the problem is likely to be found among the following six factors:

1. Fear of consequences. What if they are wrong in the decision? What if the course of action they choose requires more than they are able or willing to do? What if they can't measure up?

2. Fear of others' opinions.

3. Conflict arising from a hidden problem is being projected onto the issue at hand.

4. Information or resources are inadequate.

5. Decision-making procedures or skills are inadequate.

6. Inadequate leadership is being exercised. Notice how the need to avoid failure appears so often as the crippler of effective effort.

Keep Pointing to the Purpose

Your most vital functions as a leader are (1) to help people clarify and understand their real purposes, objectives, and goals; and (2) never to allow people to lose sight of them. Keep reminding people of why they are here and the direction they are to be moving. Keep the overall picture before them constantly. Show them how each activity is important in achieving the objectives. Be the catalyst through which God may awaken and reawaken His people to their high calling.

Weekly meetings for teachers and officers are commonly found in the most vital and fastest growing congregations. This practice provides a means for constantly keeping the vision before officers and teachers who, in turn, keep it before the rest of the congregation. It pulls many activities together with a common focus seeking shared goals.

Reinforce Desired Behavior

Leaders should understand the process of reinforcement. When a behavior is linked with satisfaction of a need or want, we tend to repeat or continue the behavior. When a behavior is linked with undesirable effects, we tend not to repeat or continue that behavior. This is the principle of reinforcement.

An example of reinforcement comes from an event in a nursery school. The children were all able to walk but several preferred to crawl. The adult supervisor preferred the children to walk, since they stayed cleaner and could participate better in activities. At first the supervisors tried to coax the crawling children to walk by lifting them to their feet and speaking gently to them. The children went on crawling and others joined them. The supervisors decided that the attention they were giving the crawlers was desirable and was reinforcing their crawling behavior. The adults began ignoring the children when they crawled and giving attention to them when they walked. Soon every child was walking.

Behavior is constantly being reinforced, consciously or unconsciously, positively or negatively. Unless they are alert, leaders may be reinforcing the wrong behaviors of the people with whom they work; they may be failing to reinforce the desired behaviors.

Be sure you are reinforcing what you intend to. The only time some church people are able to make others know they are alive is to engage in some disruptive behavior. When they do so, they receive attention, and the behavior is reinforced. How much better to recognize and honor people when they are participating constructively. Even when approximations of appropriate behavior are made or there is movement in the right direction, reinforcement will help motivate still further and better efforts.

Understand Basic Needs

Motivation is related to the "drive cycle." Drives are basic physiological or psychological requirements. Some examples of such basic drives are:

Physiological (biological requirements)
Recognition (being needed, approved, appreciated)
Possession (ownership)
Understanding (being understood as well as gaining insight)
Security (material and emotional)
Position (status, significance)
Personal fulfillment (achieving one's potential)
Companionship (association with others)

Responsibility (accepting obligations)

Clear conscience (meeting one's code of ideals)

Accomplishment (achievement, attainment of challenging goals)

Close friendship (intimate social relationships with select individuals)

Orderliness (things fit and make sense, rationality)

Drives set cycles in motion similar to the following diagram:

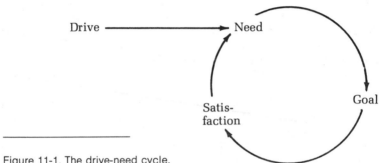

Figure 11-1. The drive-need cycle.

The drive sets up a need to be satisfied. Satisfying this need becomes a goal to the individual. When the need is satisfied, the person experiences well-being until the satisfaction wanes and need again develops.

Every person has needs that he strives to satisfy. It is entirely within the framework of Christian ethics to show people that their legitimate needs can be met through helping achieve Christ's objectives. An effective leader motivates people by enabling them to see this congruence.

In the church, we should not ignore these drives and their subsequent needs. Being a part of the human makeup, drives may be used by the Holy Spirit, just as other capabilities or characteristics are. Common drives are shared by us all but in varying strengths, depending on the individual. A particular drive may be strong in one person, weak in another. Each person has his own "profile" of strong and weak drives. Effective leaders understand their own drive pattern and the patterns of the people with whom they work.

Summary

Apathy is usually the result of one or more of the following conditions:

1. People do not see the task or activity as important.
2. The desire to protect self (from criticism, for example) outweighs the challenge.
3. People see no clear way to proceed and are discouraged.
4. People are not convinced anything significant will result from their efforts.

Effective leadership offsets all four conditions. A leader is a booster, an optimist, a challenger, a builder of morale and enthusiasm.

Effective leaders are motivators of their fellow workers. Learning to motivate other Christians to serve Christ's cause is one of the greatest challenges facing Christian leaders.

People work best when:

—They are committed to a high purpose.
—They see opportunities to work toward it.
—They realize they can make a significant contribution.
—They have a plan of procedure.
—They feel they have the necessary encouragement and support.
—They receive feedback on their progress.
—They sense they are part of a team effort.

The common idea that success spoils people by making them vain, egotistical, and self-complacent is erroneous; on the contrary, it makes them, for the most part, humble, tolerant, and kind. Failure makes people cruel and bitter.

—W. S. Maugham

For Further Reading

Bormann, Ernest and Nancy. *Effective Committees and Groups in the Church.* Minneapolis, MN: Augsburg Publishing Co., 1973. Teaches the dynamics involved in communication and leadership within small groups. Good outline of material with summary reviews after each section. Provides questions and projects for learner involvement. Helpful as a resource for task group concerned with development of leadership skills.

Dale, Robert D. *To Dream Again.* Broadman Press.

Dayton, Edward R. and Ted Engstrom. *Strategy for Leadership*. Old Tappan, NJ: Revell, 1979.

Engstrom, Ted. *The Making of a Christian Leader*. Grand Rapids, MI: Zondervan, 1976.

Gangel, Kenneth O. *Competent to Lead*. Chicago: Moody Press, 1974.

Hyde, Douglas. *Dedication and Leadership*. Notre Dame, IN: University of Notre Dame Press, 1966.

Johnson, Douglas W. *The Care and Feeding of Volunteers*. Nashville: Abingdon.

Kilinski, Kenneth and Jerry Wofford. *Organization and Leadership in the Local Church*. Zondervan, 1973.

Robinson, Jerry W. *Series on Community Development and Human Relations*. University of Illinois at Urbana Champaign Cooperative Extension Service. Booklets 1-11. While written from a secular perspective, these booklets are excellent digests of many aspects of leadership theory. The ideas are well illustrated and applied.

Schaller, Lyle E. *The Change Agent*. Nashville: Abingdon, 1972.

Schaller, Lyle. *The Pastor and the People: Building a New Partnership for Effective Ministry*. Nashville: Abingdon, 1973.

12

Plans and Strategies

As you read, think about these questions:
—What characteristics must a church have for successful planning of programs?
—How does one diagnose a congregation?
—How does one diagnose a community?
  What are the steps in developing a program once a diagnosis has been made?

Planning is a powerful factor in individual lives and in the corporate lives of congregations. Without planning, we can only *react* to circumstances, much as a thermometer reacts to the temperature of a room. Through planning we can *act*, more like a thermostat that changes the temperature of the room.
Every activity or event related to the life and work of a congregation (sermons, lessons, board meetings, committee meetings, youth meetings, men's meetings, women's meetings, Bible studies, special campaigns, worship services), and every function of a congregation (evangelism, pastoral care, benevolence, education, missions, stewardship, worship), should be pursued through careful planning. When a congregation focuses upon its reason for existence, all such events or functions take on a clearer meaning as they converge on common objec-

tives. The congregation may also discover that new strategies must be added if it is to accomplish its purpose fully.

A capable contemporary leader has recounted his boyhood experience playing checkers with his grandmother and the lessons she taught him in the process. He would make several moves, naively thinking he was getting ahead. Suddenly she would sweep the board in a series of lightning moves. While he was making individual moves that seemed opportune to the moment, she was carrying out a long-range strategy.

Unfortunately, few congregations have clear long-range plans or even short-range goals. Lacking such strategies, a congregation is likely to be passive. Its activities consist of random procedures that have haphazardly grown up. Its actions are based on vague assumptions or a scattered sense of need rather than on clear objectives. It tends to be programmed more by pressures of the moment than by God-given purposes. Boards, committees, and other functional units go their own ways with little overall, church-wide direction.

Specific, goal-oriented actions are called programs. *Program planning* is a systematic procedure for designing the ways and means to reach objectives. Program planning consists of common sense elements and appears deceptively simple. Nevertheless, essential steps are often bypassed. For this reason most leaders need to learn and follow a step-by-step procedure of program planning. Such a procedure is outlined in this chapter.

Foundations for Program Planning

If congregations are to engage the present moment most productively for Christ, they must establish certain conditions as foundations for intelligent planning and action, including the following:

1. *Maintain elasticity in ways and means.* A congregation must be able to change the shapes and forms of its programs while holding its purposes inviolate. It must be ready to adapt in those areas of discretion in order to be productive. It must develop ways that do, in fact, accomplish what God wants. God prescribed few forms; but He did give an exact purpose and the freedom to develop ways and means, guided and empowered by His Spirit.

2. *Begin to study the congregation and the field* where it is to carry out its Lord's Commission. Study of the congregation

identifíes its needs, and study of the field identifies opportunities and conditions that must be taken into account in planning strategies. Lacking firm information in these areas, churches and their leaders are often mystified by the circumstances within and around the congregation. They may act on the basis of inaccurate impressions, fall victims to decision error, "know" many things about the congregation and its field that are not true, function only at the level of intuition, and operate in a fog of generalizations and defensive thinking.

3. *Become future oriented.* Human beings tend to think of the future as if it already existed "out there," predetermined and waiting for us to arrive. They hope it turns out to be what they want, but do not sense that they can help to cause it to be so. Christ's people must begin to realize that they can help *create* the future by what they do with the Commission they have been given. All too often churches plan for yesterday by simply continuing existing programs.

4. *Raise up leaders for growth.* Most churches have trained their leaders to maintain routines, handle present situations, carry out customary activities, and react to conditions after they arise. Churches must begin to encourage their leaders to diagnose needs, discover opportunities, set goals, and develop means for achieving them.

A procedure for program planning is represented in Figure 13-1. The diagram describes the procedure at the congregational planning level, but it can also be used by subgroups, such as committees, within the congregation. The three major phases of the model are: basic clarification, diagnosing the congregation and community, and developing the program.

Basic Clarification

If we could first know where we are and whither we are tending, we could better judge what to do and how to do it.

—Lincoln

Planning begins with the ends to be achieved and works backward to ways and means. In making plans, one should first identify, clarify, or sharpen his awareness of God's purpose for the church and identify the specific objective to be reached through the program at hand.

Clarification is not a process that can be done once and for all time. It must be repeated again and again, especially at the beginning of every planning endeavor.

A description of the clarification phase is, in essence, a summary of Part One of this book. That section of the book will help you work through the process of clarifying purposes and objectives so that you can help your congregation do the same.

Congregations and their leaders often leap over this step, assuming these matters are self-evident or thoroughly understood. They are inclined to look for simple solutions rather than spend the time and effort probing the roots of problems or needs and creatively developing solutions. They look for packaged answers. They want to begin with ways and means, programs and procedures; to see what other congregations are doing and copy the programs that seem to be working. "Somebody," they feel, "must have found a shortcut we can follow, a program we can simply plug into our situation. What's working this year? What's the latest sure cure?"

Simplistic solutions, however, are usually disappointing. Purpose loses the power to direct when it is taken for granted. Most effective strategies are "homemade," laboriously and prayerfully hammered out for a given time and place.

This first phase in program planning involves such questions as:

1. *Why are we here?* The answer to this question should be a statement of purpose, couched in terms that are clear and meaningful to the specific congregation. And the statement must be congruent with the Biblical Commission. In most congregations, honest attempts to answer this question will reveal two facts: a lack of clarity and a lack of unanimity about purpose. Behind stock answers and cliches, hidden purposes often cloud the issue.

If a congregation is to become vital and effective, it must have consensus on a statement of purpose. And that statement must be so precise that it dictates procedural objectives to be identified in the next question.

2. *What are we supposed to be doing?* An adequate answer to the first question leads to the answer to this one. But as with the first question, widespread ambiguity regarding this question exists in congregations today. Varied and conflicting answers and a multitude of private objectives for the church would be found if we could assess the thinking of individuals in many congregations.

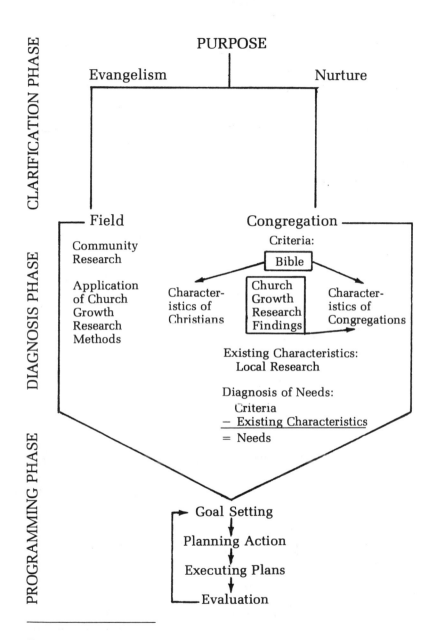

Figure 13-1. Program Planning Procedure

This second question deals with objectives: What functions are made imperative by our purpose? What things must we do in order to fulfill the purpose? What are our priority tasks?

The basic objectives as defined in this book are evangelism and nurture, along with their various components.

Clarification of purposes and objectives is a function that must go on all the time in a congregation, but it is especially crucial as a specific phase in the planning process. A congregation must have strong expressive leadership to help it come to grips with these foundational issues, readjust ideas and attitudes, and set its sights properly.

In addition to the usual preaching, teaching, and other communication functions, various spiritual enrichment and study experiences can help clarify purpose and objectives: retreats, seminars or workshops, visits to vigorous congregations, and small groups meeting for study, discussion, and prayer.

The church growth movement of the last quarter-century has made significant contributions to helping Christian leaders sharpen their awareness of the Lord's expectations. Church leaders and members alike can find in contemporary books a rich variety of resources. Those listed at the end of this chapter are of particular value for establishing a Biblical base that will lead to determined efforts to fulfill God's intentions. These books are recommended as first readings in church growth literature.

Diagnosing the Congregation

At this point in the program planning procedure, a congregation has identified the purpose and objectives it is supposed to accomplish. And it has identified characteristics that will help it succeed. The next step in the diagnostic phase reveals to the congregation where it is now and what some of its needs are. The key diagnostic questions are: Where and what ought we to be? and Where and what are we now? The equation for identifying needs is:

$$(criteria) - (existing\ conditions) = need$$

A need is the difference between where one is and where he ought to be in terms of a norm.

When a physician diagnoses a patient, he measures various

physiological functions and compares his findings with the norms for good health. A healthy person has a certain temperature, pulse rate, blood pressure, and the like. When the measurements do not match the standards, the physician has found an area of need. He diagnoses the ailment and prescribes for its cure. In a similar fashion one can examine a congregation and compare the findings with the criteria of "health" necessary if the church is to be productive in Christ's cause. The points of discrepancy indicate needs. Since needs are likely to be numerous, they must be ranked according to priority. Some needs may be more urgent than others, or some may have to be met first before others can be dealt with.

First, therefore, we must determine the criteria for congregational "health." What must we be, as individual Christians and as congregations, if we are to achieve our objectives and fulfill our purpose? What norms or standards must we meet if we are to function productively?

One way to answer these questions is through careful study of the New Testament, asking: (1) What would a Christian be if he were everything he ought to be? and (2) What would a congregation be if it were everything it ought to be? These characteristics then become Biblical criteria or ideals. Part Two of this book identifies one cluster of such criteria.

For congregational criteria, research from church growth studies provides useful insights. For example, much has been learned about the effect of building space, Christian education methods, communication, and organizational dynamics. The Bible provides qualitative ideals; research provides empirical criteria for effectiveness. The literature of church growth should be seriously studied by church leaders. Books that will help establish principles and provide insights for diagnosing conditions in the congregation are listed at the end of this chapter.

The leaders (and preferably the entire congregation) should develop and agree upon a clear list of characteristics they will seek to foster in the congregation. These norms should be kept before the congregation consistently and become standards for constant reference.

The key to diagnosis is getting the facts and the "feel" of the congregation as it really is. Donald McGavran, the prime mover in church growth thinking, calls this "rightly discerning the body."[1] McGavran properly points out:

To be sure, no one was ever saved by statistics, but then no one was ever cured by the thermometer to which the physician pays such close attention. X-ray pictures never knit a single broken bone, yet they are of considerable value to physicians in telling them how to put the two ends of a fractured bone together.

Similarly, the facts of growth will not in themselves lead anyone to Christ. But they can be of marked value to any church which desires to know where, when, and how to carry on its work so that maximum increase of soundly Christian churches will result.[2]

In church growth concepts, three kinds of questions are raised in order to examine a congregation: What is its growth history? What is the present condition? What is its potential?

1. *What is the congregation's history of growth?* Gathering and charting statistics on the size of the congregation over a period of years will reveal patterns of growth or decline. Once determined, an even more important question can be answered: What has *caused* the pattern? Virgil Gerber's volume *God's Way to Keep a Church Going and Growing* deals with methods for studying the growth record of a congregation in preparation for planning for increased growth.

A related question deals with the source of growth. Have additions to the church come from children of member families, by transfers from other congregations, or from evangelizing the true outsiders? McGavran calls these types of growth biological, transfer, and conversion growth. Research indicates that most congregations should experience a twenty-five percent increase in size in a decade through biological growth alone. When church leaders get such hard data before them, they can see their actual track record, devoid of the fog of impressions, rationalizations, and defensive thinking. Often they find they have not been perceiving conditions accurately.

For example, a congregation of one hundred members had fifteen additions in one year. They congratulated themselves; this was a fifteen percent increase in one year! Then they found that five of the fifteen came by transfer of membership. Of the ten baptisms, six were due to biological growth; only four conversions from outside the congregation had occurred. They also found that during the year, seven people had died, eight had transferred away, and five had become inactive and left the church. This amounted to a loss of twenty people and net loss of five percent. When leaders considered the six biological additions (who were not really new to the congregation) they concluded that the technical loss for the year was eleven percent (not the fifteen percent growth they thought had occurred).

2. *What is the congregation's present condition?* A demographic analysis will describe the church's membership in terms of percentages of male and female, various age levels, and various segments of society (socio-economic, occupational, educational). This descriptive information will allow leaders to compare these profiles with community population profiles to see where the church is strong or weak in reaching the community.

A geographic analysis showing where members live reveals the pattern of impact the church has made on the community and where the bridgeheads are for further reaching the community.

A program review will reveal how well provision is made for various age groups and other special-need segments of the congregation and community. It is also important to discover patterns of member involvement and participation in worship services and in such functions as classes, circles, auxiliaries, study programs, and music groups.

An examination of the budget will show where the real priorities of the congregation are. How a congregation spends its money is probably the single most revealing source of information about the philosophy by which it operates. Churches often find they are really structured for non-growth and invest little of their resources in accomplishing the purposes they avow as most important.

An evaluation of buildings and facilities will show whether the congregation is equipped to do its work well and whether it has room for growth.

One stream in the church growth movement looks for areas of strangulation or places where the congregation restricts the possibility of growth. Factors where strangulation frequently occurs include:

a) Social stratification. Congregations are often sealed off from elements of the population around them. Their memberships are measurably lacking in certain age levels (such as young marrieds or older citizens) or in certain socio-economic segments of their society.

b) Inadequate provision for leadership. Growth is related to continued addition of salaried equipping ministers. At crucial levels of growth, churches must add staff members or growth will level off. The unpaid leadership often fails to be representative of various age levels or other identifiable segments of the congregation, thereby limiting its effectiveness with the whole congregation. Growth also requires the formation of new classes and other groups; this in turn requires additional teachers and leaders. Balance must also be present in the expressive-instrumental and maintenance-task functions of leadership.

c) Group life. Maximum personal growth of members requires that they be integrated into some unit of the congregation other than corporate worship services. These units include study groups, classes, service groups, committees, choirs, and the like. If these groups are inadequate either in number or in quality, and if members and new people are not being properly integrated into them, growth of the congregation is impaired. Growth requires the constant addition of such groups.

d) Space and facilities. Functions such as worship services cannot grow if the physical space is filled. As existing events approach saturation, more space or additional events (as in the case of multiple worship services) must be provided. Failure to do so is a common source of growth strangulation.

Diagnosis of present conditions also seeks to find out where people are in terms of spiritual characteristics, personal needs and problems, attitudes, values, commitment, relationships, abilities or gifts, and reaction to what is being done in the congregation. Leaders can accomplish this through perceptive observation and listening for clues in every activity and conversation. They can also use systematic data-gathering procedures such as questionnaires. The more a leader understands the people—what they know, what they think, what they do, and how they are growing—the more intelligently he can help them fulfill their role as the people of God.

When considering these factors, churches should not stop with existing needs. They must go beyond present minimum requirements in order to create a dynamic vacuum for growth.

3. *What is the congregation's potential?* Every church has areas of strength and opportunity. Unless leaders identify and focus upon them, they may remain unused. No diagnosis is complete without an audit of such potential with a view to turning latent resources of the church into disciplemaking strength.

Assessing past and current effectiveness need not be interpreted as threatening. It should be viewed as essential insight for establishing future direction. As a spacecraft moves through space its path is charted with reference to certain fixed points such as stars. It constantly receives information about its position relative to these reference points. As the data indicate deviation from course, the craft makes corrections. Otherwise it would miss its objective. Congregations must have criteria as reference points; they must constantly examine where they are relative to these criteria, and they must take the necessary action to keep themselves on target.

One further detail of diagnosis should be considered: differentiating between symptoms and problems. A physician may observe that a patient has an elevated temperature and a high white cell count in the blood. These are symptoms. The question is *why* the patient has these symptoms. The physician then must seek to identify the underlying problem; treating the symptoms is inadequate.

One of the errors made by church leaders is the tendency to treat symptoms rather than probe for the underlying problem. The result is a frustrating process of constantly seeking to reduce troublesome symptoms that persist because the basic problem has never been identified and corrected.

Diagnosis is something like peeling away the layers of an onion. The diagnostician observes a condition and asks why it is so. When he finds an answer, he asks again why this should be so. When he has carried out this process to the point that he can find no further underlying reason, he has probably identified the real problem. When he has dealt with this problem, the troublesome symptoms will likely also be resolved.

Diagnosing the Community

A congregation must develop a clear understanding of the community that represents its primary field. McGavran calls this phase of diagnosis "rightly discerning the community."[3] This must be done because, as McGavran says, "The church must press out into every segment of society by fellowships, Christian cells, and new churches until a much larger proportion of the American people confess faith in Christ, become disciples, and live as responsible members of his church."[4]

Diagnosing the community involves identifying the community and describing it.

1. *Identifying the community.* The church is concerned with evangelizing anyone it can reach, anywhere that person may be. However, a congregation will have a specific geographical area that represents its primary field of responsibility. That area may be marked by distance alone or it may be defined by physical boundaries such as a river, a mountain ridge, or an ocean. In cities, freeways, railroads, or industrial areas create physical boundaries. Psychological boundaries also mark off communities or sub-communities. A congregation may have secondary fields into which it can also reach, but the primary community is its most likely ministry area.

2. *Describing the community.* The better the leaders of a congregation understand their primary ministry area, the better they can develop ways to gain a bearing for the gospel. Important characteristics of communities include: population growth and decline patterns; future projections for population size, economics, and culture; profiles of the people in terms of age, family structures, income, occupation, education, and ethnic groupings. United States census data and community planning agencies provide such information. Through community leaders and agencies, direct surveys, and observation, one can become aware of the population's lifestyles, values, problems, and needs.

Church growth research emphasizes the importance of understanding the culture of a ministry area. In the early days of modern missions, the missionaries tended to transmit their home cultures along with the gospel into their fields of service. The result was counterproductive, because potential converts confused the foreign culture with Christian truth. More recently missionaries have understood that the essence of Christianity should be made appropriately indigenous to the culture into which it moves, forming linkages that will enhance communication, understanding, and credibility. Still more recently American Christians have begun to realize that they face the same challenge in reaching the "cultural mosaic" in their own communities.

Jesus and all He represented were alien to the world as it had become because of sin. Yet He entered the culture of first-century Palestine, lived in the homes, wore the clothing, ate the food, spoke the language, and partook of the daily life of the people. The Word was clothed in the flesh and culture of man in order to reconcile men to God. He was in culture, yet alien to it, and used culture to relate to human beings. His uniqueness was clothed in the familiar and the understandable. This relationship is delicate. Christianity is alien to the world but must exist in and make use of the cultures of the world for God's purposes.

One gains credibility in a culture as he appropriately identifies with that culture. In the eyes of the others, he earns the right to be heard as he develops rapport with them. During World War I, Lawrence of Arabia went to the Arab nations to rally them to the cause of the Allies. The Arab leaders told him that if he expected the Arab people to follow him, he would have to live in the tents, wear the clothes, and eat the food they did. We human beings tend to respond most positively to that person who is "one of us."

Paul expressed a high level of ability to identify with other people—a quality the church ought to emulate:

> Though I am free and belong to no man, I make myself a slave to everyone, to win as many as possible. To the Jews I became like a Jew, to win the Jews. To those under the law I became like one under the law (though I myself am not under the law), so as to win those under the law. To those not having the law I became like one not having the law (though I am not free from God's law but am under Christ's law), so as to win those not having the law. To the weak I became weak, to win the weak. I have become all things to all men so that by all possible means I might save some. I do all this for the sake of the gospel, that I may share in its blessings.[5]

If the church is to evangelize effectively, it must identify with the culture around it. It must be perceived as understanding and caring about the people around it—how they think and feel, where they hurt, and what they need. The church should be a living demonstration of how Christianity works in a given culture, how people live God's way and do His work in this set of circumstances.

One of the most important elements of culture is language. The gospel must use the language of man in order to communicate God's message to the people who use that language. But culture involves much more than language, and these elements too must be taken into account. Other major cultural factors include: time, length, and format of meetings; frame of reference out of which they think and understand; styles of expression, music, dress, and buildings; norms of social interaction. In many of these factors churches follow traditions that grew up in the rural American culture of the eighteenth and nineteenth centuries or during the Renaissance and Protestant reformation in Europe. The church must ask whether these factors fit productively into the current setting, whether they communicate understanding, whether they enhance persuasion, whether they help these people identify with the message of Christianity. Congregations today in such places as Beverly Hills and Harlem should be the same in purpose, nature, and message; but in such cultural factors as those listed above they may, and probably should, differ widely.

Programming

Once purposes have been clarified, needs of the congregation have been identified, and opportunities in the community have been studied, programs for nurture and evangelism can be developed. Leaders must develop commitment to God's purpose in the congregation. They must also channel that commitment into productive vehicles; they must translate ideas into programs whereby they can be fulfilled.

Some of the resources available to help in planning and administering programs are recommended at the end of this chapter.

The following questions guide the planning of ways and means:

1. *What are our goals?* A goal is a verbal picture of the state of affairs a person is trying to achieve. The importance of adequate goals is difficult to overstate.

The previous steps must now be translated into specific goals, or the effort will have been wasted. The success of future efforts depends on the adequacy with which goals are established.

Suppose a person has the goal of becoming an expert marksman. He has a standard: the standard of performance that qualifies one as an expert marksman. He compares his present performance against the standard and sets a goal for improved performance. He practices, receiving feedback on this progress by examining the targets at which he has fired. He continues to practice until he has achieved the level of proficiency that he had set as his goal. His goal measures his progress. It motivates him to persist in practice. It guides his actions for improvement, and indicates when he has met the standard.

Goals are the means of turning dreams into reality. Adequate goals must be clear and specific. They must indicate what can be done to reach them and provide a measure by which to evaluate results.

2. *How can we reach our goals?* This question deals with ways and means—how to get from where you are to where you want to be. It calls for the following procedures: analyzing the problem into its component parts, determining the resources required, establishing a sequence of actions, assigning responsibilities and defining roles, marking checkpoints and arranging for course corrections, and devising an evaluation process to measure outcome against the goal.

The plan should be carefully written out, specifying who is in charge of each area of responsibility, listing beginning and completion dates for every component of activity, and indicating when and how evaluation is to be made. Then a launch date is set, thorough preparation made, and the program is launched.

3. *How are we doing?* This is the checkpoint question. Internal guidance is an essential component of space vehicles that probe the universe. It is not enough to aim the vessel and fire. The craft's course must be constantly monitored and, when necessary, corrected to be sure the intended goal is reached.

Programs should have built-in checkpoints so progress can be monitored, problems detected, and course corrections made. One should expect to make corrections, adjustments, and improvements as programs are carried out.

4. *How did we do?* This question tells you how near you came to your goal. Evaluation helps you identify what you did well so the skill may be called upon again. It also helps you identify errors to avoid the next time.

Evaluation is the weakest point in many programs. Because of our inherent insecurity and defensiveness, we human beings tend to shy away from putting our efforts up for examination.

Evaluation, however, is a vital link in the programming process, not only because of what it teaches us from experience, but because it cycles us back to the diagnosis and goal-setting stages for the next item in our long-range plan.

Conclusion

Programming is more than a way to accomplish particular tasks. It is a process for setting the church in continuing motion in the direction of fulfilling God's purpose. It is a skill that must be learned. The procedure may seem difficult and time consuming the first time through, but proficiency develops with practice. Committees, boards, and congregations can learn these skills—but not by accident. A winning football squad does not just happen. It develops through training and practice. Building an effective spiritual problem-solving team is at least as challenging as building a winning athletic team, and far more important.

Programming must be kept in the context of the big picture, so that details do not become disconnected from the fact that they are part of an overall strategy for reaching the highest possible level of competence in serving the cause to which God has commissioned His people. Therefore, the procedure must not operate at a purely human level or in a mechanical fashion. It must function in a climate of prayer that saturates every fiber of the activity with the power and guidance of God.

For Further Reading

Basic Clarification
McGavran, Donald A. *Understanding Church Growth*. Grand Rapids: Eerdmans, 1980 revised edition.
McGavran, Donald A. and Winfield Arn. *Back to Basics in Church Growth*. Wheaton, IL: Tyndale, 1981.
Tippett, Alan. *Church Growth and the Word of God*. Grand Rapids: Eerdmans, 1970.

Diagnosis
Gerber, Vergil. *God's Way to Keep a Church Going and Growing*. Glendale: Regal, 1973.
McGavran, Donald A. *Understanding Church Growth*. Grand Rapids: Eerdmans, 1980 revised edition.
McGavran, Donald A. and Winfield Arn. *Ten Steps for Church Growth*. New York: Harper and Row, 1977.
Schuller, Robert. *Your Church Has Real Possibilities*. Glendale: Regal, 1974.
Wagner, C. Peter. *Your Church Can Grow*. Glendale: Regal, 1976.

Programming

Arn, Winfield. The Pastor's Church Growth Handbook. Pasadena: Institute for American Church Growth, 1979.

Engstrom, Ted and Edward Dayton. The Art of Management for Christian Leaders. Waco, TX: Word, 1976.

McGavran, Donald A. and George Hunter. Church Growth Strategies That Work. Nashville: Abingdon, 1980.

Schaller, Lyle E. Effective Church Planning. Nashville: Abingdon, 1979.

_____. The Local Church Looks to the Future. Nashville: Abingdon, 1968.

_____. Parish Planning. Nashville: Abingdon, 1971.

Additional Resources

Hunter, George G. The Contagious Congregation. Nashville: Abingdon, 1979.

Peters, George W. A Theology of Church Growth. Grand Rapids: Zondervan, 1981.

Schaller, Lyle E. Planning for Protestantism in Urban America. Nashville: Abingdon, 1966.

Smith, Ebbie. A Manual for Church Growth Surveys. Pasadena: William Carey Library, 1976.

Wagner, C. Peter. Our Kind of People: The Ethical Dimensions of Church Growth in America. Oak Park, IL: John Knox Press, 1979.

---

[1]Donald A. McGavran and Winfield C. Arn, *Ten Steps for Church Growth* (New York: Harper and Row, 1977), p 61ff.

[2]Donald A. McGavran, *Understanding Church Growth* (Grand Rapids: Eerdmans, 1980 revised edition), p. 94. Used by permission.

[3]McGavran and Arn, *op. cit.,* p. 74ff.

[4]*Ibid.,* p. 93.

[5]1 Corinthians 9:19-23

CHAPTER

13

Change Does Not Have to Be a Nightmare

As you read, think about these questions:
—What are some of the reasons people resist change?
—How does a typical congregation react toward a need for change?
—How can a change be introduced to a congregation in such a way as to encourage its adoption?
—How can one "mature" an idea for change among church leaders?

Change: a word to make the bravest Christian leader quake in his boots.

But if the church is going to do a better job in the future than it is at present, then we are faced with change.

One might expect that change would be natural to an institution that deals in change (both in individuals and in the world) and exists in a world where the only certainty is change. But this has not been the case with the church. It is often one of the strongest citadels of resistance to change. In some ways this is good, because the church's essential characteristics do not need or permit change. Yet to fulfill its mission, the church must be flexible enough to develop strategies to meet the challenges of many cultures in a fluid world. The success of program planning depends to a great extent on the ability of the church to change.

Man is ambivalent toward change. On one hand we see the need for change; on the other, we prefer to cling to the familiar and the comfortable. Change presents unknowns; if we can barely manage now, how can we be sure we will be able to cope with the new? Within each of us a "yes" seeks growth and improvement, and a "no" seeks security. As bad as Egypt was, in some ways it seemed preferable (in the eyes of the Israelites) to the unknowns of the wilderness, and the wilderness seemed preferable to the unknowns of the land of promise.

People also confuse change of strategies with change of doctrinal commitment. One author calls this "morphological fundamentalism." Because both traditions and Biblical practices existed from our earliest memories, we forget the differences between them. Both are lumped together as sacred, and, therefore, untouchable. Anything new is automatically suspect—even if it more effectively achieves Jesus' purpose than the forms our grandfathers invented.

We flounder in the quicksand of traditional attitudes and expectations because we are afraid to examine them. The searing light of Scripture and reason might reveal to us a mandate for change, and we are afraid we will not be able (or willing) to carry it out. We become defensive at a suggestion for change, since it implies criticism of the way we have been functioning. Therefore, we protect ourselves by perpetuating the activities in which we feel competent. We resist the idea of change—even at the risk of refusing to do the will of God—as did the religious officials of Jesus' day.

The curator of a museum explained the disappearance of the dinosaur as its inability to turn the corner when history did. The New Testament shows disciples struggling to accept the new ways Jesus instituted, and a church struggling to accept the changes that Christianity required.

As Christian leaders, how can we help guide necessary change in an orderly and creative way? How can we cope with it and help others do the same?

The Change Process

Phases of Change

The process by which change occurs is consistent, following ten identifiable phases:

1. *Unawareness of need.* Satisfied people do not change. If a

person is unaware that change is warranted, the idea never occurs to him. The fact that a need for change is pointed out to us does not guarantee we become really aware of that need.

2. *Vague awareness of need.* A person develops a diffused and generalized awareness that all is not as it should be. He is not sure where the need for change exists, but is vaguely dissatisfied with the present situation.

3. *An area of need is identified.* This stage represents a fork in the road. If the need is correctly identified, the process of change moves in a healthy direction. The awareness of need, however, may attribute the problem to the wrong source and attempt to change the wrong thing.

In the church, leadership is often misidentified as the object for change. Dissatisfaction may be directed toward an individual—the minister, for example. We sense a need for change; therefore, we probably need a change of ministers. Ministers sensing a need for change begin to think that a different congregation may be the answer.

The need for change might not at all reside where people assume it does. The diagnostic phase of program planning helps assure that the correct area of need is identified. It helps us avoid a "scapegoating" process in which we blame persons when we should be identifying and solving problems.

4. *Nature of need becomes clearer.* As information is gathered and the situation is considered, the need for change becomes more sharply defined.

5. *Uncertainty or retrenchment.* At some point along the change process, people may have a change of heart because of fear, uncertainty, or defensiveness, and they regress. The idea of change sounds great until the awful question "How?" arises: How would we go about making the change? Where are the necessary skills and resources? People are often overwhelmed by the feeling that they do not have the slightest idea how to go about implementing the change. Such uncertainty aborts many potential changes.

6. *Rejection, postponement, or foot dragging.* Nearly every idea that is ultimately accepted first goes through rejection. Even ideas that are not rejected may be held in abeyance for a long time. The lag between preliminary acceptance and implementation is often lengthy. It is sometimes difficult to work up courage to make the plunge.

7. *Fear and postponement recognized.* If people are willing

openly to discuss the change, their courage becomes stronger. People recognize and face their fears. They realize they have been procrastinating. When information is accumulated the change seems more feasible, because people begin to see possible ways of carrying it out.

8. *Commitment.* Enough people finally come to the point of saying, "We'll do it!"

9. *Planning the change.* This is the same as the program planning procedure (see Chapter 12).

10. *Implementing the plan* so the change occurs.

A lag will probably occur between the time someone perceives the need for change (Stage 2) and implementation (Stage 10). Not everyone becomes aware of the need for change at the same pace. While some people are at the commitment stage, others are still at the unawareness stage, and the rest are scattered along the stages between.

Attitudes Toward Change

The change process usually follows a curve along a time line. For a long period of time, only a few people accept the proposed change. Then follows a period of rapid acceptance by the majority. Finally, over a long period, the last remaining holdouts one by one accept the change. The shape of such a curve corresponds to three general categories of the ways people react to change (any change): innovators, static members, and inhibitors.

Innovators are searchers. They constantly want improvement and are on the lookout for ideas. They are willing to try a change that promises progress. They are not necessarily impetuous, but are sensitized to the idea of change and respond to an opportunity quickly. Innovators are likely to be goal-oriented. Compared with people in the other two categories, innovators tend to be younger, better educated, less provincial, more well-traveled, more likely to participate in numerous activities, more active in seeking information, and less rooted in the existing system (this is a generalized profile, to which there are many exceptions). Usually, innovators comprise no more than 10% of a given group.

Static members account for about 80% of a group. These people neither actively oppose change nor actively seek it. They tend to be cautious and skeptical.

Inhibitors openly resist change. Their characteristics tend to be opposite to those of innovators. They represent about 10% of a group, but they are a vocal minority and exert an influence far out of proportion to their numbers. Many traits of human nature and organizational behavior work on the side of the inhibitors, so that they occupy a position of greater advantage than the innovators do.

One might conclude that change has a slim chance of occurring. But other factors like the mobility of populations, crises that confront people with choices, modern communications that provide exposure to new ideas and views, all can work in favor of change. The characteristics that mark innovators are becoming more prevalent in our society and in the church.

Guidelines for Change

When resistance to change is encountered, the problem may stem more from the way the idea was introduced than from the idea itself.

Even though a proposed change seems sure to increase the church's effectiveness, little will be gained if by imposing we alienate the congregation. We must operate within congregations in such a way as to help them become effective spearheads for Christ's cause.

Assuming that a change is needed and that a proposal is valid, the following guidelines will help to secure acceptance and implementation of the idea.

Begin With Purposes and Objectives

Until the purpose and objectives of the church are clear and broadly accepted in the congregation, little can be done to introduce valid changes. Once such acceptance is achieved, the people can be shown where the present conditions are not what they ought to be. The challenge and hope of serving Christ's cause can arouse people from self-satisfaction and create in them a sense of need for improvement. This realization of need can be brought about within a congregation by its expressive leadership—the leadership that helps clarify and maintain commitment to the church's purpose. Such leadership must hold up the ideals and implications of the Word as norms to be taken seriously.

Change is difficult to impose. It must come as a result of

personal spiritual growth of church members, which leads them to an overriding commitment to Christ and frees them to become dynamic participants in the dynamic fellowship of His kingdom.

If you can develop a reading, studying, thinking people who can discuss ideas openly—an informed people—you are developing creative people. The better informed people are, the better they can make intelligent decisions. People are better prepared to function in the church if they are Biblically literate, able to differentiate between Scripture and tradition, and exposed to stimulating and creative ideas.

But not only must people be educated. They sometimes must be led to change their very patterns of thought. True change must first come in the basic understandings, values, and perceptions of the people involved, not in superficial attitudes and actions. It must come in the way people see the church and themselves, and in their willingness to move in the appropriate directions. It must be more than simply a matter of changing old machinery for new.

Lloyd Ogilvie illustrates how the thinking of the church must be repatterned. A youngster in Ogilvie's neighborhood suffered brain damage in an accident, and could no longer walk and run with the other children. The doctors explained to the boy's playmates how they could help "repattern his brain." They taught the playmates to move the boy's limbs so that "new grooves would be formed in the brain" to take the place of the damaged neural paths. Dr. Ogilvie describes the joy the whole neighborhood experienced when the lad could walk, run, and play once again. The major task of our day, Ogilvie concludes, is to "repattern" the mind of the church so it can function as it was intended.

Work constantly for spiritual growth. Build the people through all you say and do. Maintain a counseling stance even in casual conversation. Function in such a role and you prepare the church for greater vitality.

Communicate Clearly

Communication in congregations is usually poor. Channels of communication—sermons, lectures, lesson presentations, and writings—have been turned into art forms by our traditions. Communications are short-circuited as these functions become exhibits of talent. Potential recipients of the communications become art critics, giving high or low marks to the performance, rather than responding to the message.

Every minister, officer, and teacher in the church should try to break this image and reestablish genuine communication that will enable members to repattern their thinking into God's intentions. But this must be done before proposed changes can be explained or understood. Members must be kept informed about *what* is going on and *why*.

Three assumptions about communication are usually valid:

1. *Assume the message did not get through.* It is estimated that 70% of what is transmitted is not received.

In life-or-death situations (such as building a craft to carry men to the moon), technical systems are duplicated. If the first system fails, its duplicate, or backup system, takes over. This is the principle of redundancy. This principle is also important in communication. A first attempt to communicate is never 100% effective. If the message is important, it is wise to provide backup systems. To ensure clarity, it is usually wise to communicate to an extent that seems adequate, and then double the amount.

Adequate communication to the entire congregation is imperative. Sometimes the leaders are so involved in the process that leads to the change, with the idea and the reasons behind it, that they forget the congregation knows much less (and perhaps nothing). They place a brief note in the worship bulletin or church paper and make a perfunctory announcement; then they wonder why the congregation is less than enthusiastic.

2. *Assume that if it did get through, it was garbled either in transmission or in receiving.*

In order to communicate an idea effectively, use every medium at your disposal. Explain it in church meetings, not once but repeatedly—using different people to say it in different ways. One approach to the subject may get through to some people, but another approach may be necessary for others. Remember the difference between hearing and *effective* hearing. *Effective* communication elicits understanding, commitment, and response.

Using more than one communications medium (posters, charts, dramatizations, written articles, and enthusiastic verbalizing) will help to get ideas through clearly.

Communication problem: *I know you believe you under-*

stand what you think I said, but I am not sure you realize that
what you heard is not what I meant.
   3. *Acknowledgment that the message was received does not
necessarily imply acceptance or compliance.*
   The most effective communication is two-way, so that feedback is provided. Feedback lets the sender know whether he
has sent a clear message and whether it has been clearly received. Insecure people shy away from feedback because they
fear it might be negative, but this attitude represents two errors.
First, feedback is more often positive than negative. Asking and
answering questions, giving further explanation, and sharing
ideas can generate creativity. Second, repressed disagreement
does not equal agreement. Hiding differences does not make
them go away.
   Discussion sessions in small groups are valuable for providing two-way communication.

   Consider two imaginary congregations. Both decide that
their evangelistic efforts are inadequate and that the people
must help in making calls. (The decision may have been made
by the minister, evangelism committee, or church board.) Visi-
tation is scheduled for Tuesday nights. This decision represents a change in both congregations
   Now look at the first congregation. The Sunday worship bulletin lists: "Tuesday, 7 P.M. Calling." Attention is called to the
schedule in the announcement period and everyone is urged to
come. On Tuesday evening, no one comes. The people who
heard the announcement did not hear effectively. The following Sunday, the congregation is reprimanded and urged to help
the next Tuesday. After several weeks of announcing, scolding,
and printing sarcastic articles (marked "—Copied") in the
church paper, three people are persuaded to appear on Tuesday.
   Now look at the other congregation. The decision was made
in the same way as in the first congregation, but now a planned
strategy of communication begins. Sermons lay the
groundwork of understanding that evangelism is the responsibility of all Christians. Posters and articles in the church paper
and worship bulletin undergird the idea. Communications are
expressed positively, optimistically, and challengingly.
   A substantial buildup is given to the first calling night. A
simple organization is set up to take the information into the

adult Sunday-school classes, women's groups, and all other church functions. The What, Why, Who, When, Where, and How are fully explained well in advance. Whenever the leaders meet people from the congregation, they say an enthusiastic word about the program. A corps of "captains" is formed to write and call church families, enlisting individuals to participate. Last minute reminders are arranged.

It is known in advance who is going to be there to call on Tuesday night. Every detail is arranged for giving instructions and making assignments. On the first Tuesday, the response is excellent, the experience is gratifying, results are seen, and the "change" is successfully established.

The difference between the two congregations is primarily one of communication.

Most congregations have plenty of activities, hold many meetings, and keep many people busy. But the people do not spend enough time talking with one another about the right things, such as dreams, aims, and plans. The meetings of teachers and officers, which are held weekly in the majority of the fastest growing congregations, are effective because they provide dependable communication.

Follow the Channels

A leader might have a sudden inspiration that he believes is an excellent idea. He announces what is going to be done, but little happens (except negative reaction). What went wrong? The idea might have been excellent, but the initiator failed to follow the appropriate steps to introduce it. If the idea involves more than a minor adjustment, requires much cooperation from other people, or falls outside of his domain of decision-making, the initiator is wise to follow appropriate steps such as these:

1. Think the idea through thoroughly. Itemize every important fact and find every flaw you can. "De-bug" the idea thoroughly, making necessary adjustments.

2. Gather all pertinent information. Let the idea mature and become more clear to you.

3. Try out the idea on a few confidants. Go through the de-bugging and adjusting process again.

4. Suggest the idea informally to opinion leaders, the individuals whose ideas carry special weight. These individuals may or may not be formal leaders or officers. Approach the

subject with such individuals, provide them the information you have, and ask them to give you their opinions at a future time. The process is the same as in the third step, but here you are building a base for support and generating more representative feedback.

5. If the idea still stands the test, take it to the lowest level of authority, such as a committee. Go through the same process as in steps three and four.

6. Take the idea through successive authority levels to the level at which a decision can be made.

7. Plan the implementation of the idea, using effective program planning procedures and involving the people who will be affected by the change.

8. Plan the means for communicating the idea to the entire congregation.

If the groundwork has been properly laid, any vote involved in the change process should be predictable. The voting should only confirm the existing consensus. If you are unable to predict the outcome, you are probably not ready to bring the proposal to a vote.

Involve as many people as possible. The more people involved in the change process, the better; the more of the process they are involved in, the better. Build the broadest possible base of support and cooperation. Provide for the widest possible psychological ownership in advocacy of the change.

Choose the Best Time and Place

One time is not as good as another. Reception to a new idea might depend more on when it is introduced than on the merits of the idea. The backwash of a totally unrelated matter can affect the response given to an idea, because of a reaction by association. Perfectly good ideas may be unacceptable because they have become associated with an unpopular idea, event, or source.

You must also allow sufficient time for others to consider your idea after you have introduced it. Avoid crash programs that stampede action prematurely. Ideas grow; like a crop, they ripen just before the time for harvesting. Give new ideas time to become comfortable; give people time to visualize them and mentally try them out before the time to decide.

Large projects or goals sometimes must be approached through a series of sub-goals or easier steps.

There are times to push for progress and times to relax and accept matters as they are. A wise man paces his innovations correctly.

The setting in which the change effort takes place also has an important effect on its chances for adoption. Important matters should not be mixed with other items on an agenda. They should be considered individually.

A neutral locale helps clear entanglements so that an idea does not become confused with other elements. An informal setting usually improves communication and open involvement. For this reason some of the most productive meetings are held in homes, in restaurants over a meal, or at a retreat facility. Departure from customary surroundings helps provide new vantage points from which to view familiar situations.

Help Motivate Proposed Changes

Show how the proposed change is in harmony with Scripture and the nature of the church. Describe its potential value in accomplishing the mission of the church. Using logically and psychologically compelling reasons, help people understand why the change ought to be made. If a change can be appropriately related to their values and commitments, people are eager for it.

A change must help to accomplish the purpose of the church and, at the same time, meet the needs of the people. The commissioned objectives of the church and legitimate personal needs can be met at the same time. This duality is extremely important in gaining acceptance for changes, and should be clearly pointed out when interpreting the proposal to the people.

If the "why" is important enough, the "how" usually can be worked out. But the "how" question sometimes strikes the mind such a stunning blow that it produces a sense of dread or a conviction of impossibility.

A minister can hold up the Scriptural ideals and show his congregation how short it falls, but if he fails to offer tangible ways to improve, discouragement and criticism can result. It may be that the people are discontented enough to be ready for a program change that will provide a way to carry out Christ's mission. But such discontent can be creative only if it is channeled into action.

One way that the paralysis of fear or negativism can be overcome is by allowing people to have a taste of the change without yet being firmly committed to it. This can be done in a workshop or retreat, through demonstration, or by a trial period.

People might see the change more objectively if they know that an avenue is open for return in case it does not work. If they understand that the change might be temporary, they will be less anxious about it, and thus the change is more likely to be successful. If the change succeeds, it can be permanently adopted.

An extensive change can be tried out with a pilot project. If you follow this procedure, make sure the right people are involved and that the project has every chance of success.

A proposed change can be introduced subtly. One minister felt that the worship service was a spiritually empty routine and wanted to inject new vitality into it. He left the order of service in its familiar form, but began to use more creatively the time allotted to him for announcements. He would use a bit of inspirational verse, tied in with a moving Scripture passage, guided silent prayer, or one stanza of a related congregational hymn (the hymn sung from memory and, of course, the musicians informed in advance). Even the age-old routines began to take on a new sense of meaning through this subtle introduction.

Another minister believed that prayer groups would add a needed dimension to the life of the congregation. A tentative suggestion of the idea convinced him that the congregation would be afraid to try such groups on a full scale. They were accustomed to spending a portion of the midweek service in prayer, however, so the minister began breaking the meeting into smaller groups for the prayer time, and suggesting specific prayer concerns. From this low-key introduction to small group experience, enough people desired more of this newly discovered prayer vitality to begin several full-fledged prayer groups.

Try to unlock proposed changes from complications. A change can be more easily made if it requires no adjustments in other activities or systems. Construct changes so that they impinge as little as possible on other systems.

For example, a group of young adults felt hindered in their Sunday-school studies. They were intensely interested and wanted more time for discussion and implementation. Changing the entire Sunday-school schedule would have been difficult, since lecturing teachers could barely fill the time as it was. A move to lengthen the Sunday-school period solely on the basis of the preference of one class would surely have failed. The class, therefore, continued using the time provided in the existing arrangement, but added a Sunday evening extension in which to carry their studies to a more satisfying conclusion. This solution resulted in no complications with other systems at that time.

The previous illustration suggests another consideration. Sometimes it is wiser to change by addition than by rearrangement of existing situations. This is not always feasible, but may be preferable.

Maintain Objectivity

If rejection of a proposed change is not intended as an attack on you, don't take it personally or defensively. If you are objective, you might find that the decision-making group has used sound judgment. It is difficult to see this, however, when you are emotionally involved in the issue.

Recognize that there may be other ways to approach solutions. Admit the problems or weaknesses in proposed changes. Show an understanding of opposite viewpoints by admitting the points at which the arguments are valid. Proceed in an atmosphere of openness, honesty, and teamwork in which the principal concern is getting Christ's mission accomplished in the best way. In such an atmosphere, the options for meeting a need should be either/or, rather than yes/no. In other words, the question should not be "Should we change?" but "What is the best change to make?"

If an idea is rejected and you are still convinced of its soundness, look to future acceptance. Remember that most changes in history were first rejected and only later accepted.

Be flexible enough to work for change when desirable and possible, but to accept present circumstances when you must.

Follow Through

Gaining acceptance for a change is only the beginning. The change will not implement itself. Make sure it is successfully implemented by giving it good programming and adequate executive attention. Many failures occur due to inadequate administration. Failure only makes it more difficult to secure acceptance for the next change.

Innovations themselves should not become sacrosanct traditions. *Ad hocricy* has advantages in this regard. A form or program is developed for *this* purpose at *this* time. From the beginning, innovations are expected to give way to further innovations if they ever become outdated or ineffective.

If the idea of reasonable change becomes the norm, it will allow our institutional forms to be stable enough to function yet open enough to adjust to changing circumstances. If gradual changes are possible, we might not have to wait until pressure builds, forcing revolutionary changes.

If we are willing to meet the challenge of bringing the gospel to today's world, we will have to be tougher in mind and spirit than we ordinarily have been. We will have to be willing to drop traditions and develop new strategies if the will of God so directs. The vitality of the church depends on its responsiveness to the directives of God, on the ability to change when necessary.

For Further Reading

Dyer, William G. *The Sensitive Manipulator: The Change Agent Who Builds With Others.* Provo, Utah: Brigham Young University, 1980.

Fabun, Donald. *Dynamics of Change.* Englewood Cliffs, NJ: Prentice-Hall, 1967.

Griffin, Emory. *The Mind Changers: The Art of Christian Persuasion.* Wheaton, IL: Tyndale, 1976.

Johnson, Douglas W. *Managing Change in the Church.* New York: Friendship Press, 1974.

Schaller, Lyle E. *The Change Agent.* Nashville: Abingdon, 1972.

Walrath, Douglas Alan. *Leading Churches Through Change.* Nashville, Abingdon, 1979.

Werning, Waldo. *The Radical Nature of Christianity: Church Growth Eyes Look at the Supernatural Mission of the Christian and the Church.* South Pasadena, CA: Mandate Press, 1975. (Management of resources, practical strategy for change in individuals and church structures, stewardship.)

Conclusion

God has given us a task; and He countenances no excuses for failure to apply our best efforts. He insists on results—as revealed, for example in Jesus' parables of the barren fig tree, the vine and branches, salt, light, and the talents.

The days ahead will call for healthy, reproducing Christians and congregations. One major denomination estimates it will have to establish as many congregations in the next twenty years as it has in the last 180 years in order to keep up with the population.

I am convinced that:

- We do not need a new church, but a restored church.
- We do not need a humanly redirected church, but a divinely directed church.
- We need empowered people more than impressive programs.
- We must not surrender to the philosophy of a shrinking church in a secular society; but we must embrace the philosophy of a living, growing church that will transform society.
- The task of Christ cannot be accomplished by the faithful few alone; every believer must be vitalized, equipped, and mobilized for ministry.

- Churches grow "not by might, nor by power, but by my spirit, saith the Lord of hosts."

We must scrutinize our work and strategies with ruthless honesty, tough mindedness, and determination to give Christ our best. Self-deceiving assumptions about our work will not suffice in place of results.

The imperative nature of our task is well-conveyed by these words:

This is not the future's first verse!
Always it keeps coming—at supersonic speeds.
Suddenly in the desert stands
　　John the Baptist.
　　"Repent!" he shouts,
　　"The future—*God's* future—is at hand!"
　　It will not wait
　　And so Jesus comes.
Are we ready?
Do we welcome Him?
Do we love Him?
Do we serve Him?
Do we see Him for who He is?
Or do we go on, hating the Romans,
Talking about the price of eggs?
Still the future speeds;
Tomorrow starts today.
　　People move.
　　Cities grow.
　　Times change.
In the name of God, we must do better than before!
The future will not wait!

APPENDIX

Section Outline

Worksheets From Church Growth Seminars

A few years ago the author conducted a series of conferences with church leaders in the Pacific Southwest. These sessions were held for the purpose of identifying current problems and needs faced by congregations and their leaders. One hundred and nine ministers and other leaders representing ninety churches met in nine cities in southern California and Arizona

Using group discussion and worksheets, the participants were asked to identify problems that hindered them and their congregations in the effective pursuit of Christ's work. They were urged to probe as deeply as possible the root causes underlying their problems, and to suggest ways the problems might be solved.

The following analysis is a composite of information gathered in the nine sessions. The expressions of the participants are represented as accurately as possible. If the descriptions appear harsh, it is because of the openness and frankness with which the participants entered into the task of seeking to expose problems and needs. Due to the purpose of the investigation, the information is by nature negative. The many strengths and successes of the participating churches and leaders are assumed but not explored in this study.

The participants were fluent in pointing out difficulties they perceived as hindering their efforts and the progress of their congregations. Probing for problems underlying these difficulties and suggesting solutions were more difficult tasks. This difficulty suggests that the processes of *problem identification, analysis, and solution* are unfamiliar to church leaders and that development of these skills is one fundamental need.

Needs of Church Leaders

As participants discussed their problems and indicated needs, the following categories were consistently named or implied. While applicable to leaders in general, these needs pertain especially to preachers.

Role Identity
Insecurity and high attrition rates among preachers are due in part to the "limbo" state of their identity. An adequate rationale and role description for the preacher in today's congregation are yet to be sufficiently developed. As a result the preacher's posture is often one of defense in the face of a bewildering diversity of duties, unclear authority, and confused expectations. Preoccupation with minutiae and the inertia of church organizational structures prevent them from addressing their time and energy to work that they consider more important. Many feel trapped in an unadmitted clergy system, in which their role is largely one of serving patrons.

Leadership
Needs in this area include: a better understanding of the nature of leadership, a more positive leadership stance in the congregation, and skills with which to exert leadership effectively. Leaders expressed inadequacies in their ability to resolve conflicts, heal divisions, and motivate the people in their congregations. They also perceived themselves as frequently directed more by emerging pressures and vocal minorities than by positive, purposeful intention.

Institutional Dynamics
Leaders frequently portrayed themselves as bewildered victims of these forces rather in control of them in a creative, productive way. Needs exist for competencies in the areas of interpersonal relations, group processes, and the nature of complex organizations.

Management and Administration

Related needs are in the areas of diagnosis, long-range projection, defining purposes and goals, identifying and mobilizing resources, programming, executive functions, and evaluation. Leaders expressed particular need for skills in recruiting, mobilizing, equipping, and deploying their people into ministry.

Intervention and the Guidance of Change

Leaders expressed frustration at their inability to cope with inertia and opposition to their efforts to turn their congregations in the direction of Biblical ideals. An understanding of the change process and skills in intervention and guidance of the process are critical needs among preachers and other leaders.

Preaching and Teaching

Also needed is improvement in the competencies involved in communicating the Bible. This area includes diagnosis and planning, objective-oriented preaching and teaching, and effective methodologies, including expository treatment of the Scriptures.

Richer Personal Spiritual Lives

Needs of Congregations

As participants discussed problems and needs in their congregations, the following categories became apparent.

Liberation From Cultural Stereotypes

Participants described congregations and individual members as locked into mindsets, assumptions, roles, expectations, practices, and participation patterns that stem more from cultural stereotypes of religious institutions than from Biblical ideals for the church.

American Protestant images of the church and the Christian life play a major, often dysfunctional role in determining the nature and function of congregations and the individuals who constitute them. Weak and confused concepts of the church divert its focus and produce strife as conflicting expectations collide. Preachers, other leaders, and general members need to understand the cultural impact on traditional church forms, understand and commit themselves to the Biblical ideals of the nature, purpose, and function of the church, and be able to judge forms and practices according to these standards.

Liberation from Institutional Processes

Under the influence of institutional processes, congregations become more committed to form than to function. Stronger allegiance is given to practices than to objectives. Perpetuation of programs is more precious than progress. As congregations become program-oriented rather than achievement-oriented, they fall prey to the activity trap in which motion is confused with accomplishment. Care and maintenance of institutional aspects of the church assume priority over the church's life and function. Success is measured against models dictated by the cultural image of the church. In the familiar means-ends reversal, forms are granted unfounded commitment regardless of their effectiveness (or lack of it). Anxiety for institutional security leads to inappropriate promotionalism and to an endless search for simple, packaged programs that will ensure success. Biblically ideal results tend to be meager compared with the investment necessary to achieve them. In order to overcome inertia, aimlessness, and weakened motivation, people are coerced into supporting programs, even when they do not perceive the programs as relevant to their needs or as dealing with the heart of critical issues.

Commitment to Evangelistic Outreach

So much time and effort might be expended on inner maintenance of the organization that outreach occurs almost incidentally. Outreach is sometimes slanted toward recruiting new persons primarily for the contribution they can make to the success of the institution.

Complacent or defeatist attitudes were described as prevalent in some congregations.

Congregations need a strong, deliberate, rational focus on evangelism, a commitment to growth, an aggressive, confident mentality, and strategy consciousness—at both congregational and individual levels. Other needs in this area include effective means for motivating, recruiting, training, and deploying large numbers of Christians into deliberate evangelistic efforts.

Knowledge and Use of Church Growth Concepts
Conditions that cause churches to be vigorous and effective frequently go unidentified. Congregations are often simplistic in their understanding of the social milieu they are attempting to engage with the gospel. Bound to identities, forms, and practices developed for social conditions that are now passing, churches are prevented from developing strategies through which to engage emerging conditions.

Inability to bridge cultural gaps reaches far beyond the racially changing urban setting. As churches fail to recognize the diversity posed by age, sex, socioeconomic levels, and educational and religious backgrounds, they become more narrowly stratified in their constituents and outreach.

Church Membership
The masses of the people in the congregations need to grasp more clearly the concepts of personal commitment, individual responsibility, high privilege, and team relationship, which include every member in the ministry of the church.

Members frequently function primarily as patrons of the church, which, in turn, assumes the role of a service-vending enterprise. Due to this relationship, many members tend to be self-seeking in their attitudes and behavior. While the masses are relatively inert, the burden of responsibility is unduly heavy for the few.

The concept of *vocation* for all Christians needs to be articulated and implemented.

Motivation
Motivating people is the single problem most often cited by participants in the conferences. This is a central need if their congregations are to be revitalized. At least five needs must be met if increased motivation is to occur:

1. *Tangible ways for people to operationalize their commitment.* People are frustrated by a global sense of responsibility, while at the same time immobilized by typical congregational structures and programs in which they find little to do but attend the services.

2. *Serious individual recruitment.* Blanket invitations or casual inquiries made in passing do not challenge people. In recruitment efforts, the importance of the task is often minimized by attempts to make it sound less burdensome.

Poor performance is a related problem. Ineffectiveness, irresponsibility, and slipshod execution of tasks has bordered on the normative in many churches.

3. *A sense of ministry.* We need to interpret service as ministry in Christ's cause. Many tasks have the appearance of organization tending. Lacking spiritual dynamic, such tasks soon become burdensome. Attempts to motivate people sometimes take the form of social pressure or of imposing a sense of guilt or obligation. When highly involved people change residence, they often refuse to accept responsibilities in the new congregation.

Traditionally, people have not been made conscious of possessing talents or "gifts;" nor have they been given a sense of privilege in employing these gifts for the glory of Christ and the benefit of the total body.

4. *Adequate orientation, equipping, and support* in the discharge of duties.

5. *Supportive fellowship.* Churches often lack the quality of fellowship that helps individuals find their best area of service, encourages them into action, and lends support to their efforts.

Effective Church Polity

Officer selection processes, roles, relationships, responsibilities, authority, and expectations need an adequate rationale, generally shared understanding, and functional acceptance. Expressed job descriptions and "psychological contracts" need the clarity and congruence of expectations that will allow congregations to function effectively. Lacking this, paralysis and conflict typically result.

Leadership has been mistakenly equated with office holding. Election to an office does not automatically bestow the skills of leadership. Officers need to be trained in how to function in their roles and how to exert leadership. Attempts at leadership training typically focus on certain of these Scriptural qualifications, but neglect other essential elements.

Biblical Literacy

The masses of church people were described as weak in knowledge, understanding, and personal incorporation of the Word of God. Ill-equipped to deal with doctrinal confusion, many people are being caught up with emerging novelties. They need the intellectual tools and motivation to study the

Bible in order to gain the competencies to express their faith, deal with questions, and cope with error.

Church educational programs are in need of serious revision. Curricula should be developed in order to meet real, diagnosed needs. Objectives should be clearly formulated. Programs should be deliberately planned and seriously executed, and should move toward developing in the people specific and functional competencies.

Despite the multiplication of meetings and activities in typical congregations, leaders do not perceive the people as being effectively equipped for life or ministry.

Spiritual Vitality

To a large extent, the churches are seen as operating on the secular or purely human level. Rather than function as a spiritually empowered body, the church looks to organizationalism and promotionalism for its continued existence and progress. On one hand, this spiritual aridity leads to disillusionment; on the other, to spiritual eccentricity. Lacking in prayer and faith, the church moves cautiously along only as far and as fast as human sight and resources allow.

In the lives of many individuals, churchmanship seems to have replaced, to a serious extent, personal spiritual vitality. Many members appear to have been won more to the institution than to Christ. They are organizationally related to the church instead of being incorporated into Christ's body as functioning members who both receive and contribute to its life. As a result, these people tend to meet only minimum institutional norms, rather than experiencing the adventure of transformation into Christlikeness.

Interchurch Relationships

Opposite extremes of opinion have been expressed about "brotherhood identity." On one hand churches were described as provincial, isolated from the broader religious world, and unaware of trends and resources in the contemporary religious scene. On the other hand, fears of a broad relativism were expressed. Leaders are concerned that doctrinal softness is causing movement toward absorption into the general evangelical sector, which operates at the lowest common denominator, and may neutralize the distinctive message, principle, and influence of the congregations.

Some leaders described their congregations as melting pots of contradictory doctrines. Individuals need an understanding of their heritage and a clearer, better integrated doctrinal comprehension.

Unconcern, strife, and competition among sister congregations were prominently cited as problems, along with local preoccupation at the expense of the church at large. Mutual support and cooperation in sharing strengths and resources were named as major needs.

Congregational Relationships

Relationships in congregations appear deficient in the quality of Christian fellowship. Congregations tend to function more as associations than as true communities. Persons function more as individuals than as fully responsible and participating members of the body. They are only partially absorbed into a fellowship of life and service. These individuals need more open, comfortable, supportive, growth-producing, motivating, norm-setting relationships. Superficial relationships, defensiveness, personality clashes, and power plays immobilize congregations, discourage involvement, isolate people, and boost attrition rates.

Communication

Despite busy schedules filled with meetings, in-depth and effective communication appears lacking in several directions: leader-leader, leader-congregation, congregation, congregation-community, congregation-college.

Facilities and Stewardship

Somewhat surprisingly, the identification of problems focused more on basic, intangible factors than upon physical concerns such as finances and buildings. The assumption prevailed that tangible needs would be met if the more basic problems could be solved. However, problems with inadequate financial resources and limited physical facilities were expressed frequently enough to warrant mention.

Exercises

Try on some of the ideas you have encountered and see how they fit you and your situation. If possible, do at least some of the exercises with a small group, discussing your responses.

Exercise 1

On a separate sheet of paper make four columns. Head the columns:

> Tradition Determines It
> Members Expect It
> Maintaining the Institution Requires It
> Biblical Ideals Establish It

Think of as many details of your congregation's activities as you can, and list them in the appropriate columns to indicate why they are done.

As a starter, list "time of Sunday morning worship service." In which column does it go? Why? Be as specific as possible.

Exercise 2

Name the church activities you might drop if you were perfectly free to do so. Name some you would add. List some changes you would make.

Exercise 3

We can gain a fresh view of familiar situations when we try to describe them in terms of unusual images. Use the form below to try to describe the church—first as you think it ought to be, then as you think it is in your situation. For example: If the church could be described in terms of a color, what color would it be ideally? What color would it be in your situation? Explain what your answer means.

If the church were a:	What do you think it ought to be, ideally? Why?	What do you think it actually is? Why?
Color		
Texture		
Shape		
Motion		
an Animal		

Exercise 4

Divide a sheet of paper into twelve sections. Number each section, and write one of the statements of concerns (shown below) on each section. After cutting or tearing these sections apart, sort them twice.

The first time, sort them according to your view of their importance: the most important concern on top, the least important on the bottom. Make a list of the numbers in sequence.

Next, sort them according to the amount of attention they actually receive in your congregation: the one receiving the most attention on top, the one receiving the least attention on the bottom. List this sequence of numbers alongside the first list.

Compare the importance of the items with the amount of attention they receive.

1. Raising and expending funds
2. Maintaining peace and harmony
3. Getting workers to fill all the jobs
4. Growth of members to function as mature Christians
5. Winning local people to Christ
6. Maintenance of buildings and grounds
7. Maintaining or building attendance
8. Meeting expectations of the members
9. Foreign missions and benevolence work
10. Meeting expectations of society or other congregations
11. Keeping the existing weekly programs going
12. Developing a sense of fellowship or mutual concern

Exercise 5

In terms of your church life, rate yourself on each item below. Using "O" as the midpoint, on which side would you be? How far? Underline the numbers that represent you.

Then score your congregation on the same scale, circling the numbers that represent it.

Connect your numbers to make a profile, then connect the congregation's numbers. Compare the two profiles.

Committed to means	4 3 2 1 0 1 2 3 4	Committed to objectives
Guided by routine	4 3 2 1 0 1 2 3 4	Guided by goals
Objectives vague	4 3 2 1 0 1 2 3 4	Objectives clear
Accept traditions	4 3 2 1 0 1 2 3 4	Examine traditions
Follow existing forms	4 3 2 1 0 1 2 3 4	Make forms fit function
Rigid in opinions	4 3 2 1 0 1 2 3 4	Open to ideas
Spiritually dormant	4 3 2 1 0 1 2 3 4	Spiritually vital
Sense of isolation	4 3 2 1 0 1 2 3 4	Sense of fellowship
Primarily solidary	4 3 2 1 0 1 2 3 4	Primarily purposeful
Satisfied	4 3 2 1 0 1 2 3 4	Searching for improvements

Exercise 6

Examine the following attitudes and relationships in the light of the discussion (Chapter 7) of Christ's purpose vs. tradition, institutional maintenance, and private purposes. What insights does the concept give you about:

- Your own attitudes?
- The nature of your congregation?
- Your relationship to other members of the congregation?
- The relationships among members of the congregation?
- The relationship of members to the congregation?

Exercise 7
Discuss how to:
- Help people understand and commit themselves to the real purpose and objectives of the church.
- Help people differentiate between tradition and Biblical norms and become willing to subject tradition to the accomplishment of Christ's task.
- Keep a balance between maintaining the institution and accomplishing the task.
- Keep incentives balanced.

Exercise 8
Select a major church activity. State what you believe its primary purpose is intended to be. To what extent do you believe this purpose determines the way the activity is carried out?

Exercise 9
Read the following statements and answer these questions about each statement:
1. Is a problem indicated?
2. If so, what do you think the problem is?
3. How might the existence of the problem be explained?
4. Does an understanding of the reason for the problem affect your reaction to it?
5. How might the problem be solved?

"Our church is dragging in a lot of new people who are not our kind. Either they go or I do!"

"The announcements always come *after* the second hymn, not *before*."

"We need to get some new members who will be good givers and hard workers."

"Fellows, let's quit talking about trivial details—like replacing light bulbs—in board meetings, and see what can be done to win more people to Christ."

"We can't have that Thursday Bible study for youth in the church. The church is always cleaned on Tuesdays and it will be all messed up for Sunday."

"We ought to start a men's fellowship in our area. Almost every area has one except ours."

"Preacher, it's been almost six months since you were by to visit me. Our last minister used to stop by real often. You wouldn't want one of the charter members of the church to feel neglected, would you?"

"I hear nearly a hundred young people are coming to the new Sunday evening program. Must be letting in a lot of outsiders. We don't have more than thirty or forty in the whole congregation."

"We want a minister who will build up the congregation to what it used to be. Why, I can remember when . . ."

"There's a lot of potential in our congregation, if the minister would get out and stir things up. We have a lot of good people. All we need is the right leadership."

"We can't add a full-time staff member to head our evangelism program. We still have to raise $30,000 for the new sanctuary furniture."

"People in the neighborhood are just not interested. A few have joined, but they are not active. Not many even visit the services, and those who do seldom come back."

Exercise 10

Analyze the following situation.

What is going on? What are the options facing the congregation? On the basis of the description, which option would you be inclined to favor?

An old congregation meets in the same building it has occupied for 75 years. Once a thriving congregation, it now consists of about ten families—all of whom drive ten miles or more to the building. Attendance averages 30 on Sunday morning. The church does not meet at any other time, since it is no longer considered safe to drive into the area at night. The youngest person in the congregation is 35 years old. Former members are scattered among several congregations in the areas where they now live. The remaining few hate to see the old home church die. They are very fond of one another and enjoy being together. Therefore, they continue to meet in their crumbling building in a now-alien neighborhood. There have been no additions to the congregation for more than five years, except the children of the member families.

How would the situation differ if the congregation had a larger, newer building on which they still owed a mortgage?

Exercise 11

In terms of maintenance vs. task achievement, which type of leader would you say you are? (See p. 138)

☐ a balanced leader   _____

☐ a taskmaster   _____

☐ a Charlie Brown   _____

☐ a bureaucrat   _____

In the spaces to the right, indicate the number of officers in your congregation whom you would classify in each of the categories.

Exercise 12
Locate yourself on the following scale in terms of which kind of function receives most of your attention.

Expressive function 3 2 1 0 1 2 3 Instrumental function

Exercise 13
How many officers are in your congregation?   _____
How many of them would you consider
                              positive leaders? ☐ _____
                                     neutrals? ☐ _____
                                    negatives? ☐ _____

List some ways you might help all the officers become more positive leaders.

Exercise 14
Make a list of the characteristics that you think an effective leader should have. Circle the characteristic that you feel is your strongest one. Underline the one you feel is your weakest. Set for yourself one goal that will help you become a better leader.

Exercise 15
Analyze the following situation.
How can you explain what happened? What errors were made by the new class? How might the problem have been averted? Once the problem developed, how might it have been solved in a better way?

In going over the church records, a minister became aware that several young couples were not attending Sunday school. As he talked with these couples, he found they did not feel at home in their Sunday-school class, since most of the people were older. Neither did they find anything in the class to challenge them.

They expressed interest in a class especially for them—a class in which they could explore seriously what the Bible had to say to them. No classrooms were available in the church building, so the minister asked the three interested couples if they would like to meet in the family room of the parsonage next door,

The couples were delighted. They eagerly participated in a serious study that began to have a profound influence on their lives. They found a new spiritual vitality through the fellowship, study, and fervent prayers in the class. They began working at projects through which they could express their growing Christian compassion. They also became evangelistically concerned. Several other couples were won to Christ.

The class grew and became vital. In order to spend more time together, they began coming earlier and did not go to the church building for the Sunday school opening exercises.

One morning the minister was encountered by an angry chairman of the elders. There was serious displeasure about that class, he was told. The teacher of the class where the young couples should have gone was miffed. The men's class was unhappy—it was no longer the largest class in the Sunday school. Some of the people were a little suspicious of what was going on in this new class; it just didn't seem right.

The class, it had been decided in an elders' meeting, was to be brought into the church building. Two children's departments had been combined to provide a room. In addition, the class was to attend the opening exercises. From now on, one of the elders was going to teach the class. So that these young people wouldn't just pool their ignorance in discussion, he was going to instruct them in basic doctrines.

Within a month, the class dwindled. In six months it went out of existence. The three original couples went back on the roster of their former class—as absentees.

Exercise 16

Analyze the following incident. What made the difference between the two congregations?

Two congregations received the same disaster appeal. In the first congregation, special offering envelopes were placed in the worship bulletins and an announcement was made urging generous response to the emergency. When the money was counted, 349 envelopes contained $1.00 each, one contained $5.00, and two contained $10.00 each.

In the other congregation, the appropriate committee met and set a goal of $1,500 to be given in one day. They explained the need to the congregation, announced the goal in advance, and reemphasized that goal on the day the offering was to be given. When they counted the offering, 337 envelopes contained a total of $1,577.

Exercise 17

Itemize the major characteristics of the ideal New Testament congregation. Then describe your congregation in terms of these characteristics. Describe your congregation as you would like it to be a year from now; five years from now. Pick one area of need and outline a program for meeting that need. Outline a strategy for implementing the program.

Inventory of Needs
for Church Leaders

Each of the following statements describes a condition or state of affairs. Does it describe you or your congregation? For each statement, circle the number if you feel that you or your congregation needs to improve in this area. Then reconsider all the items you have circled and number them according to priority for attention.

____ 1. I clearly understand the purposes and objectives of the church.

____ 2. I am able to increase my competence in church leadership through a program of continuing education.

____ 3. I am able to identify the causes of problems in my congregation, especially the non-theological causes.

____ 4. I am able to develop strategies for eliminating the causes of problems that hinder my congregation.

____ 5. The congregation and I understand clearly the scope of my authority and responsibility in carrying out the work of the church.

_____ 6. I am able to relate the content of Biblical preaching to the goals and programs of my congregation.

_____ 7. I am able to lead in the planning and administration of programs to meet specific goals.

_____ 8. I have good relationships with the people in the congregation.

_____ 9. I am able to resolve interpersonal conflicts by redirecting people toward goals.

_____ 10. I am able to motivate our members to service.

_____ 11. I know where to find outside help for solving problems, and meeting needs.

_____ 12. I am able to recruit, equip, and deploy members into goal-oriented tasks.

_____ 13. I am able to harmonize the organizational structure of the church so that we move directly toward the defined goals of the church.

_____ 14. I am able to help my congregation make necessary changes in our programs.

_____ 15. I have a supportive, stimulating relationship with my fellow preachers.

_____ 16. In addition to public presentations, I am able personally to win people to Christ.

_____ 17. The positions and functions of the officers in our congregation are understood and accepted by the general congregation.

_____ 18. Elders, deacons, boards, and committees in our church understand that they exist to help reach new people for Christ.

_____ 19. The elected officers of the church see their major task as helping others work for Christ effectively.

_____ 20. Our church conducts regular in-service retraining in goal-oriented church leadership for all the officers.

_____ 21. The organizational structure of our church minimizes interpersonal friction.

_____ 22. Program difficulties are viewed not as failures, but as opportunities for feedback for reprogramming.

_____ 23. The officers of our congregation understand how organizations function. They exert the kind of leadership that moves us toward our goals.

_____ 24. The congregation is constantly adding new classes or groups that play an active part in the church.

_____ 25. The church is constantly developing leadership for the new classes or groups that are created.

_____ 26. The buildings and equipment of the church are constantly expanding to allow the addition of new classes and groups.

_____ 27. Our congregation understands the relationship between the number of paid staff and our church's growth potential.

_____ 28. Our congregation constantly evaluates its activities in order to effectively carry out Christ's purposes.

_____ 29. The church readily abandons programs that do not promote growth.

_____ 30. The church members see themselves as unpaid coworkers with the paid staff in carrying out the mandate of Christ.

_____ 31. Each individual church member knows what "gift" of ministry he possesses and uses it joyfully in the life of the church.

_____ 32. Our people demonstrate lives marked by prayer, faith, and the fruit of the Spirit.

_____ 33. Our worship services are planned, Spirit-filled, and effective in reaching our goals.

_____ 34. Our Christian education program is built to meet the needs of our own local situation.

_____ 35. Our Christian education program equips our people to act effectively as agents of Christ.

_____ 36. Our people take the initiative and find tangible ways to put their commitment to Christ into action.

_____ 37. When a person is given a responsibility in our church, we are confident that he will perform on a consistently high level.

_____ 38. Our people practice stewardship in such a way that needed activities are adequately financed.

_____ 39. Our church understands and is committed to the restoration of the Biblical model for the church.

_____ 40. Our congregation is committed to the worldwide mission of the church in terms of recruits and money.

_____ 41. Our people understand the differences among biological growth, transfer growth, and conversion growth.

_____ 42. Our congregation feels a responsibility for the welfare and success of its sister congregations.

_____ 43. The rank and file of the church personally study the Bible and are able to discuss intelligently major Biblical doctrines.

_____ 44. The people of our congregation are able to use the Bible to convey the gospel to non-Christians.

_____ 45. Our people understand the field of apologetics and are able to defend rationally attacks on the Christian faith.

_____ 46. Our people individually use sound principles of Biblical interpretation in order to draw valid conclusions.

_____ 47. Our people are able to discriminate between Biblically mandated functions and those that are traditional or institutional.

_____ 48. Our people realize the Holy Spirit wants to lead the church into dynamic growth.

_____ 49. Our people are vitally committed to the primary duty of reaching the lost for Christ.

_____ 50. Our congregation develops leadership and programs to meet specific needs of the non-Christians in our community.

_____ 51. The church gives more concern to outreach than to the maintenance of the institution.

_____ 52. New converts are put to work immediately in systematic outreach.

_____ 53. The church concentrates on winning the friends and relatives of the recently saved.

_____ 54. The church tends to concentrate upon reaching one homogeneous unit, or one socioeconomic level, in the community.

_____ 55. The leaders of our congregation know how to analyze our community for outreach efforts.

_____ 56. There exists in the church a free, positive, and open exchange of ideas and cooperation in developing and executing programs.

_____ 57. Our people are bound together in a fellowship marked by deep caring and concern.

_____ 58. In the families of our congregation, togetherness is based on each member's participating in building Christ's kingdom.

_____ 59. Our congregation adequately uses resources provided by colleges, camps, associations, and in-service training programs.

_____ 60. The growth of our people as individuals toward Christlikeness is obvious.

Index

Scripture Index